Architecture of the Old South

SOUTH CAROLINA

Architecture of the Old South
SOUTH CAROLINA

MILLS LANE

Special Photography by VAN JONES MARTIN

Editorial Assistance by GENE WADDELL

Drawings by GENE CARPENTER

The Beehive Press SAVANNAH · GEORGIA

Frontispiece: Drayton Hall, 1738–42.

Library of Congress Catalog No. 84–70059

Contents

SOUTH CAROLINA

This volume begins a series of books about the historic buildings of the Old South. Each volume will illustrate and describe the important and beautiful buildings of one or two states in a sensible chronological and stylistic order, all set in a brief cultural and social framework but without any attempt to make a preachy architectural thesis. Just as every student, including this one, leans on the researches of others, this book is intended as a framework for further study.

There have been many books about American architecture but few recent serious ones about particular states. Survey books too often illustrate the same famous buildings, some of which their authors may have never seen in person, repeating the same observations and some of the same errors, easily selecting didactic examples, and imposing a grand, if artificial, orderliness on the subject. Every student knows South Carolina's most famous buildings—Goose Creek Church, Drayton Hall, the Miles Brewton and Nathaniel Russell houses. But how many know Archdale Hall, a Palladian-inspired building a generation earlier than Drayton, or Robert Mills's Circular Church in Charleston, which antedates his other more famous domed churches, or The Elms, an amateur's Jefferson-inspired country house, or Milford, a Greek Revival temple copied page by page from one of Minard Lafever's pattern books, or James Frazier's fabulous Gothic octagon?

The Civil War represents the triumph of industrialization, homogenizing the nation's cultural life and beginning the end of regionalism in American architecture. But, despite this series' title, *Architecture of the Old South*, buildings throughout America were always probably more alike than they were different. The great architectural styles of early America—colonial Georgian, Adamesque Federal, the Greek Revival and Gothic Revival—were international movements. Many of the greatest buildings of the South were designed by professionals from outside the region or copied from builder's pattern books published in London, Boston, Philadelphia or New York, often for newcomers from New England, a group whose contributions to life and architecture in the Old South have been generally overlooked.

Indeed, upon a close look at the architecture of one state, the forces of localism seem stronger than regionalism. The special cultural and economic factors shaping one prosperous community, one influential patron and his admirers or one talented craftsman and his apprentices often created clusters of buildings with distinctive plans and decorations. In South Carolina, some outstanding local types are the "single houses" of Charleston with their many-galleried side piazzas, the tabby mansions of Beaufort, the double-entrance dwellings of Upper St. John's and the gracefully arcaded porches of Edgefield County.

Buildings are three-dimensional history books which reflect the comings and goings, successes and failures of real people. South Carolina's early architecture is extraordinarily fine, because it was an old, well-established and prosperous colony. After the Revolution, the young state, enriched by rice and cotton, continued to produce notable buildings. But after about 1835, when settlers began to head from the old states of the coastal South to the fertile new lands of the Mississippi Valley, South Carolina's architecture declined in quality. As we explore more of the Old South in future volumes, like pieces in a puzzle, we will begin to appreciate the relationship between the history and buildings of the old, well-established coastal states, Virginia, the Carolinas, Maryland and Georgia, and the rougher frontier states, Tennessee, Alabama, Mississippi and Louisiana, as well as the region's contribution to American architecture.

The plans, elevations and sections drawn for this book are all (with the exceptions of those on pages 36, 113 and 115) reproduced in the same scale to facilitate comparison of the relative size of buildings. The scale is indicated below the plan on page 13. Unless otherwise noted, plans show the principal floor of each building. Drawings are by Gene Carpenter and architectural photographs are by Van Jones Martin unless another source is indicated.

In April, 1670, some 150 colonists settled on a neck of land at the west bank of the Ashley River of Carolina. These colonists carried with them eighteen months' supply of food, clothing, Indian presents and other equipment, including six sets of carpenters' and joiners' tools, hammers, saws, wedges, augers, locks, hooks, hinges, nails and one thousand bricks.[1] Seven years before, Charles II had granted the territory between Virginia and Spanish Florida, the southern part of which would later become South Carolina, to eight political supporters. These Lords Proprietors offered prospective colonists cheap land, commercial concessions, limited self-government and freedom of religion. The northern part of the colony, early settled by Virginians, was given its own separate government in 1712.

Protected by creeks and marshes on the water side, the colonists dug a defensive ditch, six feet deep and four to ten feet wide, across the point. They cleared nine acres of land and built a star-shaped palisade fort. Settling farms a mile or two up the river, they planted corn, peas, wheat and ginger. In 1672 Antonio Camunas, a Spanish soldier, reported that there were already thirty houses built at the settlement on Albemarle Point.[2] The first temporary shelters were probably improvised huts made of upright saplings bound together with vines and sealed with clay against water and wind. These dwellings must have been extremely small, for in 1671 the authorities admonished colonists to make their houses "twenty foot long and fifteen foot broad at least."[3] In March, 1671, it was reported that there were "200 and odd souls" in Carolina, four hundred by January, 1672, some six hundred by 1675 and one thousand by 1680. In 1680 the province of Carolina still consisted of the village at Albemarle Point and small farms along the banks of the Ashley and Cooper rivers and other nearby waterways.

In 1680 the main settlement, which had been named Charles Town, was moved to higher ground at the end of a peninsula across the Ashley River. (In 1783 the name of the city was modified to Charleston.) The original settlement had begun as a haphazard village of hastily assembled huts, but the new town was an instant city, laid out according to a plan provided by the Proprietors and constructed rapidly by the many people who had already come to the colony. Now the Proprietors ordered that some dwellings of the new town should be "thirty foot long and sixteen foot wide and two storeys and an half high" and built on land far enough above the high water mark so "that there may be convenient cellars made under ground."[4] By March of that year the Proprietors received word that some twenty houses had already been

I.
Colonial Beginnings, 1670–1740

erected, that ten were under construction and that eighteen more would be finished in three months.[5]

In May, 1680, Maurice Mathews, a surveyor who had come to Carolina ten years before, wrote: "The Town is run out into four large streets. The court house, which we are now building, is to be erected in the middle of it, in a square of two acres of land upon which the four great streets of 60 foot wide do center, and to the water side there is laid out 60 foot for a public wharf."[6] Most of Charles Town's first buildings extended along East Bay, facing what was then a marsh. When Thomas Newe reached the village in May, 1682, he recorded: "The town, which two years since had but three or four houses, hath now about a hundred houses in it, all which are wholly built of wood, tho' there is excellent Brick made, but little of it."[7] In 1704 the city was bounded on the south by marshes and Vanderhorst Creek (later Water Street), on the north by creeks (now Market Street), on the east by the Cooper River and on the west by fortifications (now Meeting Street). When the Cooper River's banks began to erode, they were reinforced with brick walls and wooden palisades, the space between them filled with "oyster shells and sodd" to break the force of the sea.

In November, 1680, sixteen vessels were lying at anchor in Charles Town harbor. In the late 17th century, Carolina shipped furs, skins and

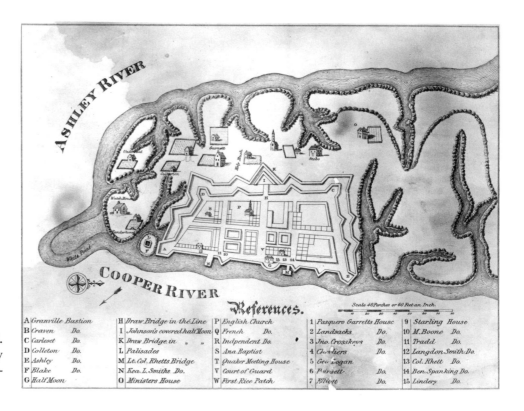

"A Plan of Charles Town from a Survey of Edwd. Crisp, Esq. in 1704," 19th century lithograph by Duval and Huter, Philadelphia. *Library of Congress*

cedar to England in return for manufactured goods and sent pitch, tar and lumber to the West Indies in return for sugar, rum and molasses. Rice, introduced in the late 1680's, rapidly became the greatest export of the 18th century. Indian traders brought furs and deerskins from the Catawba, Cherokee, Creek, Choctaw and Chickasaw Indians from as far away as the Mississippi River. The principal path from the Indian nations came into Charles Town down a road which later became King Street. The shippers and merchants were located on the Bay, where wharfs, called "bridges," projected into the river. The end of the Ye-massee War in 1717 removed at last threats of Indian invasion, and when Carolina became a crown colony in 1729 it began to flourish under a more stable colonial administration. Between 1700 and 1740 Charles Town doubled in area and tripled in population. By the 1730's there were 3000 people and 600 houses in the town.

In 1682 Samuel Wilson, secretary to one of the Proprietors, had advised future colonists to bring with them "an axe . . . for every man, and a cross-cut saw to every four men, a whip saw and a set of wedges . . . to every family . . . as likewize nails of all sorts, hooks, hinges, bolts and locks for their houses."[8] The Carolina colonists came from a pre-industrial England, a small, rural country whose domestic buildings were still constructed along medieval patterns. London was a city of wooden houses until the great fire of 1688. These boxlike frames of rough-hewn timbers were not self-consciously designed but built according to tradition and habit. Until the end of the 18th century, the traditional great hall of medieval English houses remained an element of house planning in Carolina. Though there were no architects as we know them, skilled craftsmen specialized in housebuilding. Among the colonists who came to Carolina during the province's first ten years were at least thirteen professional builders—carpenters, joiners, saw-yers, plus two ship carpenters.[9]

Joseph Moxon (1627–1700), an English hydrographer and mathe-matician, described housebuilding techniques probably used during the early years of the colony in his *Mechanick Exercises*, published in in-stallments after 1694. The house frame rested on a simple foundation wall made of three, four or five brick courses laid on the ground. Large timbers for the walls were shaped into long rectangles with a broad axe and smoothed with an adze. It might take thirty great timbers, each fifteen by twelve inches thick, to assemble a small four-room, two-story house. Pine, plentiful and easy to saw, was the favorite colonial building material for these house frames. In 1710 Thomas Nairne advised the colonists: "After having cut down a few trees . . . whilst some servants

Late 17th century building tools, from Joseph Moxon, *Mechanick Exercises* (London, 1694). *Houghton Library, Harvard University*

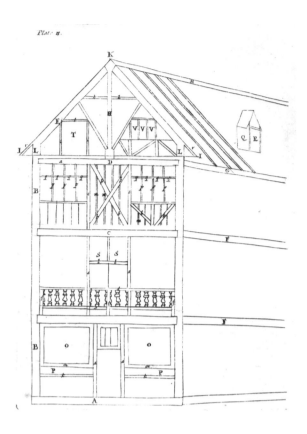

are clearing the land, others are to be employed in squaring or sawing wall-plats, posts, rafters, boards and shingles."[10]

The heavy timbers of the house frame were fitted together with mortise-and-tenon joints and held in place with wooden pegs, a technique which would be used till the second quarter of the 19th century, when lightweight, machine-milled lumber and cheap, factory-made nails became available. Each timber fitted together with a chisel, mallet and auger, the skeletal frame and roof of a building was much like the hull of a ship turned upside down, a mechanical structure which had become a work of art in the necessary care with which each part was carved and joined. Many of Carolina's first houses were surely made by the same carpenters who also made ships. The upright studs of the walls were filled with straw, clay, brick, stone or marsh grass. In 1725 Mrs. Margaret Kennet wrote to her mother in England: "As to the buildings in Charles Town they are of Brick, Lime, and Hair, and Some Very fine Timber Houses."[11] A law of 1717 refers to buildings "of Brick, Wood or Wooden Frames."[12] By the latter, the legislators probably meant half-timber construction—a timber-framed house with the spaces between the timbers of its walls filled with bricks, stones or other material. (Fortunately, a late example of this early construction in Charleston, probably built by Dr. Samuel Wilson about 1818 at 4 Magazine Street,

A house of half-timber construction at 4 Magazine Street, Charleston, early 19th century. *Carolina Art Association*

was photographed before its destruction.) The roofs were covered with thatch or shingles. Clapboards were split from logs about four to six feet long. The log was first split into quarters through its length, then further split radially into slender wedges. Chimneys were made of brick or a combination of wood and clay.

Inside these houses great structural posts and beams stood out from walls and ceilings, sometimes boxed in with smooth boards. Interiors were often whitewashed, doors and wainscot were made of flush boards, and windows were casements of diamond-shaped panes held together with lead joints. After about 1700, sash windows began to be used. Margaret Kennet wrote in 1725 that Charles Town's buildings were "generally glazed with shash window[s] after the English Fashion."[13] But evidently lead casement windows were still being used in September, 1736, when an Irish woman in Charles Town was struck by lightning: "It passed under her Chin, over her right Breast, and burst her stays on the right side. . . . Several boards were ripp'd from the House, many panes of Glass broke, and the Lead melted in divers places."[14] Ironware, tools, nails, roof tiles, paving stone, window frames and fancy carved marble mantels were all imported. Thomas Nairne reported in 1710 that ships brought "nails of all sizes . . . and all kinds of iron-ware."[15]

Middleburg Plantation, Huger, c. 1697.

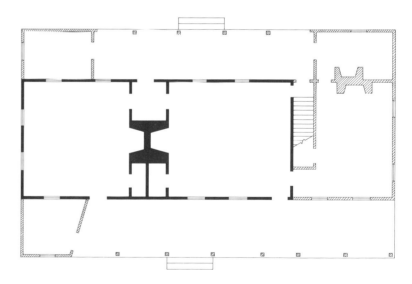

Benjamin Simons, a Huguenot planter, is believed to have built Middleburg Plantation on the south side of the Cooper River near the hamlet of Huger about 1697. This hip-roofed, two-story frame structure is probably the oldest dwelling in Carolina, with exposed timber-framed construction and a simple two-room plan common in colonial Carolina. The insides of the exterior walls are plastered, but the heavy corner posts and girts of the frame project into the room. Originally two rooms shared a single chimney, but the house was enlarged in the 18th century. Partitions are simple vertical boards, but the interior was partially redecorated in 1825.

The fortifications around Charles Town were made from vast quantities of bricks, most of them locally produced. The first colonists had brought bricks with them probably to build chimneys and foundations, but they were soon making good bricks for themselves. About 1709, John Lawson wrote that Charles Town had "good buildings of Brick and Wood, and, since my coming thence, has had great additions of beautiful, large Brick buildings."[16] In 1713 the colonial Assembly required that all new construction within the lines of fortifications must be built of brick. Along with naval stores and rice, bricks were common productions of plantations along the Ashley and Cooper rivers, where good clay, firewood for kilns and easy transportation were readily available. The 400-acre plantation at Cainhoy offered for sale by James Sandiford in December, 1747, was "good for Rice or Corn, and making of Bricks."[17] It is true that bricks were brought to Carolina from England and New England, but this was because cargoes coming to Charles Town were generally lighter than those going back and ships needed ballast which could be sold, not because bricks were unavailable locally.

Medway, Cooper River, 1705. Late 19th century photograph shows the building somewhat enlarged but before the addition of Romantic stepped gables. The plan shows the original building. *Carolina Art Association*

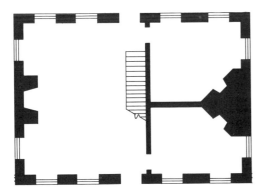

Medway Plantation on the Cooper River was famous for its brick production. The house on the property is probably the oldest brick structure in South Carolina, though not as old as traditionally reported. When Edward Hyrne came to Carolina from Lincolnshire, England, in 1700, he purchased Medway, with "the best Brick-house in all the Country, built about 9 Years ago . . . 80 Foot long, 26 broad, Cellar'd throughout," indicating that it had been built about 1690.[18] But in January, 1704, this old house was destroyed. Elizabeth Hyrne wrote her English relations in March, 1704: "We was burn[ed] . . . out of all, our house taking fire I know not how in the night and burned so fircely that we had much to do to save . . . beds just to lye on. . . . Cloes and every thing, nothing, escaped the fire."[19] A new brick house, core of the present house, was probably built the following year. This house was advertised in the *South Carolina Gazette* in 1738: "a good brick house, 36 feet in length, 26 feet in breadth, cellars and kitchen under the house."[20] Today this building has been completely obscured by changes and additions, including romantic stepped gables added in the late 19th century.

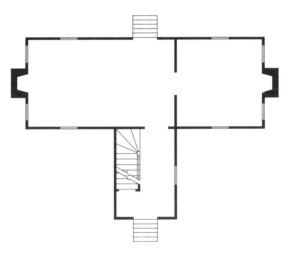

Ashley Hall, Ashley River, c. 1704. Watercolor by Charles Fraser, 1803. *Carolina Art Association*

Ashley Hall, a plantation on the Ashley River, was established by Stephen Bull, who had come to Carolina in 1670 with the first English settlers, and owned by his descendants until 1870.[21] The two-story brick house is believed to have been built about 1704 by his son William Bull, Lieutenant Governor of the colony from 1738 to 1755. About 1800 a third story was added and the building was stuccoed. The house burned in 1865, after further changes had been made, but we know its early appearance from a watercolor sketch made by Charles Fraser. Ashley Hall was notable for two elements of its plan. First, the principal story had one large oversized room flanked by a smaller adjacent chamber, an American cousin of the all-purpose great halls and their adjacent screened passageways of medieval English dwellings, which continued to be the heart of the English house as it evolved in the 16th and 17th centuries. Second, a stair tower projected from the main body of the house, a medieval arrangement which persisted into the reign of James I in England and continued to be a feature of Carolina buildings throughout the colonial period.

St. Andrew's Church, Ashley River, 1706–08, rebuilt 1764. Watercolor by Charles Fraser, 1800. *Carolina Art Association*

In 1704 the Church of England was made the established faith of Carolina, and churches became extensions of the provincial government, levying taxes, assisting the poor and supervising elections. The colony was to be divided into parishes, and soon construction of parish churches, paid for with public funds, was commenced. The typical 18th century Carolina church was a one-story, rectangular, stuccoed brick building with round-headed windows, a hipped or jerkinhead roof, usually without a tower. In plan, the chancel was at the east end, with a cross-aisle in the middle. St. Andrew's Church, built on the Ashley River outside Charles Town between 1706 and 1708, is the oldest Anglican church building in South Carolina. Built by Thomas Rose and John Fitch, whose initials are carved in the red tiles of the floor, St. Andrew's was originally a forty-by-twenty foot building, stucco over brick, with arched windows. A steeple was planned but never erected. Choir and transepts were added in 1723. After the church was gutted by fire in 1764, the interior was rebuilt and then again remodeled in 1855.

In the late 17th century, England had undergone rapid, if sometimes erratic, social and economic changes which pushed a small, rural, traditional country to the threshold of international prominence and the industrial revolution. Holland was the richest and most progressive nation in Europe, with a fleet of ships twice the size of England's, and had an important influence on English architecture. At the end of the century, English Royalists retreated to Holland during the Revolution and adopted Continental ideas about building, elements of lively Baroque design and hipped roofs, and several Dutch inventions, including stepped gables and the weight-and-pulley mechanism for sash windows. South Carolina's early 18th century architecture reflected the variety, richness and contradictions of English architecture in this era of rapid change.

St. James's Church, Goose Creek, was begun in 1708 and completed about 1719 to serve a congregation of powerful Barbadoes planters who settled in the area in the late 17th century and were the dominant group in the colony during its first thirty years. Barbadoes, first settled a half century earlier, had become overcrowded by the late 17th century. A Barbadoes planter, Sir John Colleton, had organized the group of Proprietors to whom Charles II granted Carolina. Lord Ashley, one of the Proprietors, had owned a plantation in Barbadoes in the 1640's and 1650's. William Hilton, a sea captain from Barbadoes, had launched the first, though unsuccessful, attempt to colonize Carolina in 1663. Sir John Yeamens, the first governor of the colony, had come from Barbadoes. Of those whose background can be traced, half of the colonists who reached Carolina during the 1670's came from the West Indies.

St. James's Church, Goose Creek, 1708–19. Watercolor by Charles Fraser, c. 1800, and view of restored exterior. *Watercolor: Carolina Art Association*

The first missionary at Goose Creek, Samuel Thomas, had been sent by the Society for the Propagation of the Gospel in 1702 to teach Negroes and Indians, and he had increased the congregation to thirty-two persons and taught twenty blacks to read before his death three years later. The next missionary, Francis LeJau, recorded the slow progress of his new church in complaining letters to the Bishop in London. He wrote in 1707: "We are making bricks." In 1710: "The building of Our Church . . . had been laid aside for a while, but they seem now with much adoe resolved to go on & design to make an end of that tedious Affair." In 1711: "I must arm myself to see neither my church nor house finish'd." In 1714: "My Church that was begun six years ago is not like to be so soon finished." In 1717: "Our old building that served hitherto for a church is quite open'd and ruin'd. But our New Church is to be finisht . . . within a few months and workmen are Actually Employed about it."[22]

The simple exterior of Goose Creek Church has a jerkinhead roof and round-headed windows, ornamented with cherub's heads on keystones. The front door has a pediment, in which is carved a mother pelican feeding her young, the emblem of the Society for the Propagation of the Gospel, and an elaborate entablature whose frieze is decorated with flaming hearts, another symbol of love and sacrifice. The richly decorated interior reflects the wealth and pretensions of the powerful Barbadian planters. An enormous Baroque reredos, made of painted plaster, stands behind the pulpit. Pairs of Corinthian pilasters support an entablature, broken pediment, scriptural tablets and the royal arms of George I. The marble tablets, bearing the Apostles' Creed, Lord's Prayer and Ten Commandments, were added in 1758. The pulpit and reading desk date from the late 18th or early 19th century. The chancel rail was installed about 1876. The front end of the church collapsed during an earthquake on August 31, 1886, and the exterior has since been restored several times, using an early 19th century watercolor by Charles Fraser as a guide.

The 1886 earthquake also destroyed Archdale Hall, another monument to the unexpected richness and variety of Carolina's early architecture and one of the colony's most extraordinary but least known buildings. Though only its foundations remain today on the north bank of the Ashley River near Summerville, photographs were made of Archdale Hall immediately after the earthquake. The Hall was probably built sometime between 1706 and 1710 by William Baker, whose family, like so many early Carolina colonists, had come from England by way of the West Indies. It was a two-story brick structure over a partially

St. James's Church, Goose Creek,
interior views. *Lower photograph:
Library of Congress*

Archdale Hall, Summerville, c. 1706–10. Photographs of the exterior and principal room were made in 1886. *Charleston Library Society*

excavated basement. The original, probably hipped, roof appears to have been replaced before the building's destruction. The elegantly composed façade had Flemish bond brickwork, glazed headers, giant pilasters at the corners with moulded brick bases and capitals, water-table, stringcourse and a projecting central pavilion with cartouche carved in brick.

Archdale Hall's interior was as splendid as its exterior. Interior walls were finished with plaster over panelled dado, but there was highly unusual plaster decoration. Over the mantel the builder sculpted a long frieze filled with a basket of flowers flanked by griffins and rocaille ornament. These motifs seem to have been borrowed from Antoine Desgodetz's *Edifices Antiques de Rome*, published in 1684. Over an arched door leading to the stair the builder carved a royal coat of arms and consoles supported by cherubim. Archdale Hall must have been designed and executed by a builder who had just come from England, for giant pilasters, projecting central pavilions and brickwork of such refinement had been first introduced in England from Holland only in the late 17th century and were virtually unknown in America before the mid-18th century. Like Drayton Hall of a generation later, Archdale Hall was a pacesetting design, the last word in architectural fashion in England and far ahead of its time in the colonies.

Mulberry, Moncks Corner, 1714. Painting by Thomas Coram, c. 1800, shows slave houses in front of the dwelling. *Carolina Art Association*

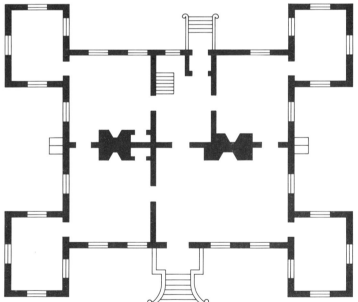

Mulberry was the home of Thomas Broughton, Lieutenant Governor of Carolina in the mid-1730's, built on a bluff of the Cooper River about three miles south of Moncks Corner. It is a building which looks backward rather than forward in style. Mulberry may have been com-

Mulberry, front and side views.

pleted before 1714, the generally assigned date, for in September, 1711, the missionary Francis LeJau wrote: "I have now no leading man or men of authority in my Parish, Col. Broughton had left us 3 months ago to go and live upon his fine seat fourteen miles off."[23] Mulberry is a brick, one-and-one-half story structure, laid in English bond with moulded brick watertable and jerkinhead roof. Four one-story brick pavilions with bell-shaped roofs project from each corner of the main block. The pavilions and the form of their roofs recall Jacobean corner turrets of a century earlier in England. Other echoes of early English building are a projecting stair tower and asymmetrical plan with a great hall. The interiors of Mulberry were remodeled in the Federal style about 1800.

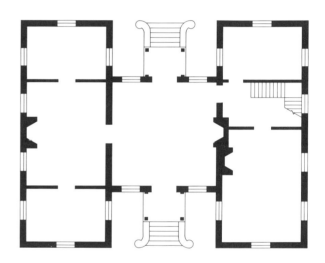

Exeter, Moncks Corner, c. 1712. Photograph, showing 19th century additions, was made in 1940, with restored view. *Photograph and restored view: Library of Congress*

Exeter, a gambrel-roofed, one-and-one-half story brick structure, was built about 1712 for Hugh Butler on the west side of the Cooper River, two miles north of Mulberry. Butler was a member of the Grand Council of the Proprietors in 1719, a member of the provincial Assembly and an Indian agent. Before it burned many years ago, the house had been considerably altered by the demolition of two wings and the addition of large projecting two-story gables, with decorated bargeboards, at the front and rear. It is believed that Exeter had an H-shaped plan, one often found in the first three decades of the 17th century in England. Parts of the walls were laid in Flemish bond with elegant glazed headers.

24

St. Philip's Church, Charleston, 1711–23. Right: Drawing by William Birch, probably early 19th century. *The Henry Francis du Pont Winterthur Museum.* Below, left: Drawing by an unidentified architect, perhaps for rebuilding of the church in 1835. *Charleston Museum.* Below, right: Painting of the interior by Thomas Middleton, 1836. *St. Philip's Church*

St. Philip's—"a new brick church at Charles Town"—was built between 1711 and 1723 to replace a decaying cypress meeting house of the 1680's.[24] Its completion was delayed by a shortage of money and damage by a hurricane, but William Bull was able to write to London in August, 1723, about "a new erected Church, not yet entirely finished, a large, regular, & beautiful Building, exceeding any that are in his Majesty's Dominions in America."[25] A stuccoed brick structure, more than one hundred feet long and sixty-two feet wide, with a cupola rising to a height of one hundred feet overall, St. Philip's had three porticoes, each with four Tuscan columns, facing the three open sides of its tower. Below a barrel-vaulted ceiling, galleries ran around the sides and rear of the interior, supported by an arcade with fluted Corinthian pilasters between the arches. George Milligen-Johnston, an army physician in Georgia and Carolina, described the interior in 1763: "The Roof is arched except over the Galleries. Two Rows of Tuscan Pillars support the Galleries and Arch that extend over the Body of the Church. The Pillars are ornamented, on the inside, with fluted Corinthian Pilasters, whose Capitals are as high as the Cherubims over the Center of each Arch, supporting their proper Cornice."[26] The church burned in February, 1835, and the following November the cornerstone of a new church, loosely modeled on the old one, was begun.[27]

Limerick, Cordesville, c. 1713.
Library of Congress

The house at Limerick, a plantation producing naval stores and rice on the northwest side of the east branch of the Cooper River, was built by Daniel Huger, son of Huguenot immigrants, about 1713.[28] Photographed before it burned in 1945, Limerick was a two-story frame

Limerick, interior views.
Library of Congress

structure with tall gable roof, a great hall, fireplace walls of the principal rooms panelled with cypress and fireplaces finished with wide bolection mouldings and shallow shelves. Cypress was a special favorite for interior panelling, despite the difficulties of sawing and transporting it, because the massive trunks of those giant trees made wonderfully wide boards.

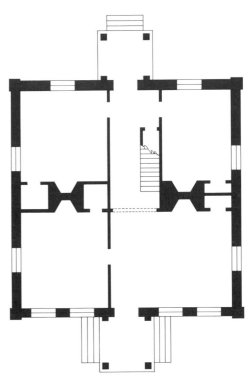

Brick House, Edisto Island, c. 1725.
Library of Congess

The Brick House at Edisto Island was built by Paul Hamilton about 1725, a two-story structure with a tall hipped roof and Flemish bond brickwork. Unusual plaster decoration was used for quoins at the corners and around window openings and as bibs under the windows. Like so many of England's houses of the period, the buildings of Carolina were sturdy, boxlike structures with wide, flaring eaves which kicked the water away from the walls and windows, stringcourses which strengthened the walls where floor joists were inserted, jack arches which supported and shifted the weight of walls above windows, water-tables which protected foundations from rainwater. Brick House was burned in 1929, but from photographs we know the interior had round-headed doors and cupboards with panelled walls finished with bolection mouldings.

Brick House, interior views.
Carolina Art Association

Crowfield, another brick house with a similar plan, is also gone. It was built about 1730 in Berkeley County by Arthur Middleton. Eliza Lucas came to Carolina from the West Indies, the daughter of a British Army officer, at the age of fifteen in 1738. She visited Crowfield about May, 1743, and described its splendid situation: "The house stands a mile from, but in sight of, the road and makes a very handsome appearance. . . . From the back door is a spacious walk a thousand foot long, each side of which nearest the house is a grass plat ennamiled in a Serpentine manner with flowers. . . . On the left hand is a large square boleing green sunk a little below the level of the rest of the garden with a walk quite round composed of a double row of fine large flowering Laurel and Catulpas . . . a large fish pond with a mount rising out of the middle—the top of which is level with the dwelling house and upon it is a roman temple. On each side of this are other large fish ponds properly disposed which form a fine prospect of water from the house."[29]

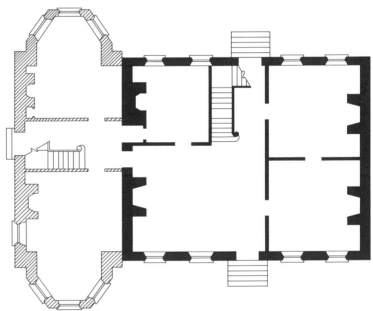

Fenwick Hall, John's Island, 1730, enlarged 1787. Photograph was made c. 1920. *Library of Congress*

Fenwick Hall, on John's Island, was built in 1730 by John Fenwick, a planter famous for his stable of race horses. The brick walls of the house are laid in an irregular bond, with watertable and modillion eaves cornice. An octagonal wing, laid in Flemish bond, was built in 1787 for a later owner, John Gibbes. When the doorway, sash and window shutters were restored in 1931, the interior was altered and a probable central hall eliminated. But this handsome building nevertheless evokes the solid, comfortable, plain but workmanlike appearance of country houses in Carolina in the second quarter of the 18th century.

Middleton Place, Ashley River, c. 1704–41.
Drawing by Paolina Bentivoglio Middleton,
c. 1842. *Middleton Place*

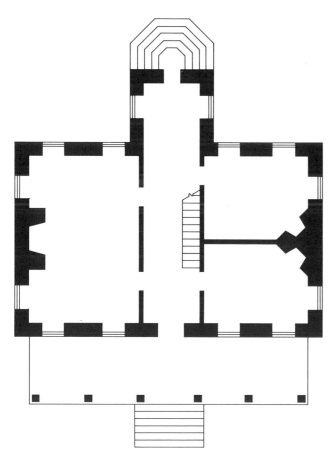

Middleton Place, plan.

Middleton Place has been the home of one of South Carolina's most illustrious families since the early 18th century. The main house, facing the Ashley River outside of Charles Town, was erected sometime between 1704 and 1741 by John Williams or his son-in-law Henry Middleton, whose father was a former colonial governor and whose brother owned Crowfield. Henry became president of the Continental Congress, the owner of some twenty plantations, 50,000 acres of land and 800 slaves. After Middleton married Mary Williams in 1741, he added flanking dependencies—a library on one side, a laundry and bedrooms on the other. When the Duke de la Rochefoucauld-Liancourt visited Middleton Place in 1798, he recorded: "The ensemble of these buildings calls to recollection the ancient English country seats."[30]

A recently discovered drawing, made by Paolina Bentivoglio Middleton about 1842, provides our first accurate glimpse of the buildings of Middleton Place, which were destroyed in the Civil War. The main house was a brick structure, laid in Flemish bond, three stories over an excavated basement, with moulded brick watertable and stringcourses, jack arches, hipped roof and entrance tower. La Rochefoucauld-Liancourt wrote: "The rooms in the house are small."[31] Today, a visitor, pacing off distances 'round the surviving foundations, will discover that, despite the splendor of its surroundings, the house itself was a small one. In plan, there was a central hall with a dining room on one side and two smaller rooms, a pantry and withdrawing room, each with a corner fireplace, on the other side of the first story. The second story had a large reception room and two smaller rooms. The third story had four small rooms. The stair from the second story led to a gallery around the walls of the third, so that visitors could look up from the second story to the ceiling of the third.[32] A long piazza, stretching across the river front of the house, was added in the 19th century. The hip-roofed flankers, with their bull's-eye windows, pediments, cupolas and weathervanes, were more self-consciously stylish than the old house. In its glory, surrounded by rice fields and its extensive gardens, Middleton Place was one of the most famous plantations along the river, a symbol of prosperity and privilege. Probably for that reason, the main house and flankers were burned by U.S. troops in 1865.

Charles Town was a real little city, described in 1739 as a "Metropolis," with accomplished builders and good buildings. But on the afternoon of November 20, 1740, a calamitous fire broke out. By the time it had been checked six hours later, the blaze had consumed about one-half of the town, most of the area from present-day Broad Street to Water Street between East Bay and Church Street. Thanks to that conflagration and other fires in 1698, 1699, 1700 and 1731, as well as later improvements to the few structures which survived, there are virtually no houses left intact from the period before 1740. The architectural historian is further embarrassed by the almost complete lack of personal papers before 1740.

Advertisements in the *South Carolina Gazette* indicate that the building trades were flourishing. The owner of "A Negro Man named Tony, a Bricklayer" offered him for hire in June, 1732.[33] In February, 1733, a slaveholder offered for sale "A Negro Man . . . named Peter, he's a Bricklayer, Plaisterer and White-washer."[34] In February, 1734, Samuel Holmes, bricklayer, offered to make "Draughts of Houses" and estimate costs.[35] In January, 1735, Charles Chassereau, "newly come from London," advertised that he "draws Plans and Elevations of all kinds of

"Charles Town, the Metropolis." Engraving by B. Roberts (London, 1739). *South Carolina Historical Society*

Buildings, both civil and Military, likewize perspective Views of prospects of Towns or Gentlemen's Houses or Plantations, he calculates Estimates for Buildings or Repairs, inspects and measures Artificer's Works, sets out grounds for Gardens or Parks."[36] In March, 1736, John Bedon advertised that he would do "House Carpenters and House Joyners work, and also makes Coffins."[37] In July, 1736, Richard Martin was doing "House, Sign and Ship-painting and glazing Work . . . after the best manner, imitation of Marble, Walnut, Oak, Cedar, &c. at five Shillings a Yard."[38] In June, 1739, Richard Baylis from London offered to do "Stone and Wood Carving and Carpenters and Joyners Work."[39]

Our one important record of early Charles Town is a view of the city drawn by B. Roberts in 1739. It shows a crowded waterfront of dwellings and offices along the Cooper River from Granville's Bastion on the south to Craven's Bastion on the north, a prosperous panorama dominated by the tower of the second St. Philip's Church. With their stepped gables and hipped roofs, these houses—a surprising number of row and double houses—remind us of a north European port. These are square, mostly symmetrical dwellings, with gambrel, double-hip and jerkinhead roofs, ornamental quoins, modillion eaves cornices, balustraded rooftop promenades and cupolas. A few buildings have doors framed with pilasters or engaged columns. If any building can be described as typical of Charles Town before the fire of 1740, as seen in this unique view, it was a two-and-one-half story brick structure with a gable, but sometimes a hip, roof, dormers and a second-story balcony across its street front, supported by turned columns. Notably, the ridges of these gable roofs run parallel to the street and there are few, if any, of the side piazzas for which the city would become so famous in the 19th century.

By the mid-18th century, rice had become the most important product of South Carolina and what Charles Mackay later called "the art and mystery" of rice planting had become an annual ritual.[1] In late winter, the fields were cleared and harrowed. In April and May, slave women, their skirts tied up 'round their hips, sowed the seed. For the next three months, the fields, controlled by dikes and gates, were flooded, off and on, to irrigate the crop, kill the weeds and support the frail rice stalks as they became heavy with the grain. From early September till the first frost, the harvest took place. In the late fall, the crop was threshed, winnowed and milled, separating the grain from the straw and husk and polishing it. From January to May, the crop was shipped, primarily to England, while the slaves began to prepare for the next year's crop. Always, the fragile rice was at the mercy of gales, freshets and high tides, which would wash out the banks of the fields and flood the plants with salt water. "May birds" in the spring ate the first sprouts, and "rice birds" in the fall ate the grain on the eve of the harvest. Fearful of malaria, the planters fled from their plantations during the summer and early fall, from June to October, to the mountains or seacoast. The house at Wigton, a 545-acre rice plantation near Goose Creek, was built by John Fraser between 1744 and his death in 1754. A watercolor drawing by his relative, Charles Fraser, pictures Wigton about 1800 and shows us the handsome but fairly simple appearance of these mid-18th century rice plantations.[2]

II. *Georgian Grandeur, 1740–1780*

Wigton, Goose Creek, c. 1744–54. Watercolor by Charles Fraser, c. 1800. *Carolina Art Association*

In 1821, Robert Mills visited Fairfield, a rice plantation on the South Santee River, home of Thomas Pinckney: "The situation of Col. Pinckney's house commands an extensive prospect of what may be called the

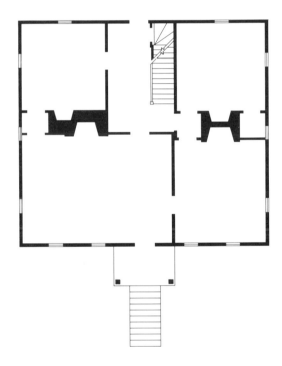

Fairfield, McClellanville vicinity, c. 1730, enlarged c. 1766.

gold mines of the state, namely the rice fields. The Santee River glides majestically by, silent and slow. A number of handsome country seats stretch alongside its banks, each fronted by rice fields. The prospect here is said to be enchanting in the spring when the young rice is shooting luxurious from its bed."[3] Fairfield was built about 1730 by Thomas Lynch, whose parents came from Ireland in the 1670's. He was a member of the provincial Assembly and grandfather of a signer of the Declaration of Independence. Fairfield was originally a two-story frame structure on a high brick basement, with four rooms on the first story and two on the front of the second story. An inscription scratched in the chimney, "January 27, 1766," probably refers to the completion of two rooms at the rear of the second story which were added by a subsequent owner, Jacob Motte. The porches were built at the end of the 18th century by Thomas Pinckney.

Hampton, which later became one of the grandest of all Carolina plantation houses, was built by Daniel Horry in the early 1730's or by his son Daniel Horry, Jr. in the late 1750's, near Wambaw Creek and the Santee River.[4] The Horrys were descended from Elias Horry, a Huguenot who, born in Paris in 1644, had come to Carolina, by way of Amsterdam and London, about 1695. The original house at Hampton was a simple frame cottage, much like Fairfield and Wigton, with a hipped, cypress-shingled roof, four rooms on the first story and two rooms on the front of the second story. The fireplace walls of the two principal rooms of the first story were completely panelled. The other walls were finished with flush vertical boards painted with a combination of stenciling and graining.

Sometime after 1768, when Daniel Horry, Jr. was married, Hampton was enlarged. The rooms of the original cottage were now plastered and papered. Two rooms were added to the north side of the second story. The lower part of the original stair, below the landing, was removed and rebuilt so that it rose from the rear of the hall. The landing remained in place, but new steps were added above the landing to provide access to the new north second-story rooms. Wings were added at each end of the original cottage. At the east end, a single "long room" extended two full stories to a cove ceiling. Its four walls were panelled with cypress, and its mantel had a shelf supported by finely chiseled consoles. On the west end, new bedrooms and sitting rooms were added. False windows, with permanently closed shutters, on the second floor of these wings gave the exterior an illusion of symmetry. The enlarged roof was covered with slate.

Hampton, McClellanville vicinity, c. 1730–50, enlarged before 1785.

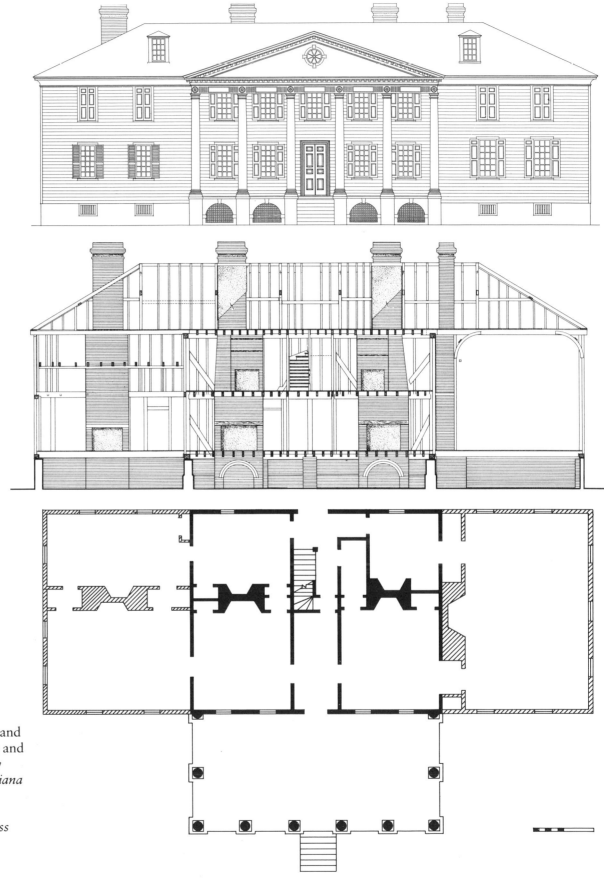

Hampton, elevation, section and plan, showing original house and its enlargement. *Elevation by Frank E. Seel: South Caroliniana Library, University of South Carolina. Section by Colin Brooker for The Beehive Press*

Hampton.
Top: Parlor of original house.
Bottom: Ballroom added c. 1768–1785.

In 1790–91, on the eve of George Washington's visit to the South, a great monumental portico was added to the south front of Hampton, supported by eight Roman Doric columns which originally rested on a floor covered with brick pavers. The portico's frieze is decorated with paterae, recessed plaques and reeded panels. On Sunday morning, May 1, 1791, President Washington reached Hampton and was, according to tradition, the first visitor to enter the house under its new portico, the final addition to a building which, like Washington's own Mount Vernon, with its long portico and two-story ballroom added to a smaller house, had been enlarged over a half century from a modest cottage into an impressive country seat. Hampton's portico was a symbol of the great prosperity of an era, for the great house had become the center of a vast 5000-acre plantation which produced rice, indigo, lumber, shingles and naval stores.

Charles Town, 1774. Painting by Thomas Leitch.
Museum of Early Southern Decorative Arts

Bored with the routine of rural life, the rice planters would spend midwinter in Charles Town, when the annual settlement of factors' accounts took place and February festivities, including horse races, were held. By the mid-18th century Charles Town had become the fourth largest city in colonial America, exceeded in importance only by Philadelphia, Boston and New York. Some 250 vessels were coming to the port each year. In 1746, eighty-six ships sailed for Europe, 121 to the West Indies and forty-eight to the Northern colonies. They brought clothes, nails, tools, beer, earthenware, paper, pewter, brass, iron and copper ware, guns, powder, mirrors, as well as roof tiles from Holland and England, slate from Maryland, New York and Wales and carried away 70,000 deerskins each year, furs, rosin, pitch, tar, raw silk, indigo and, above all, rice. Georgetown, a rich rice district on the Peedee and

Santee rivers without a deep water port, sent its crops to Charles Town on its way to Europe. Beaufort, to the south, had an excellent harbor but was located inconveniently on an island and too close to the Spanish in Florida. Cainhoy on the Wando River, Moncks Corner and Childsbury on the Cooper, Dorchester and Ashley Ferry Town on the Ashley, Rantowle's on the Stono and Jacksonborough on the Edisto all funnelled their produce to Charles Town. In 1751 James Glen wrote: "Cooper River appears sometimes a kind of floating market, and we have numbers of Canoes, Boats and Pettyagues that ply incessantly, bringing down the Country Produce to Town and returning."[5]

By 1770, there were 5030 whites and 5831 blacks in Charles Town, a city defended by one hundred cannon and seven batteries along the Cooper River. Fortifications on the landside had been begun in 1757, intended to guard the peninsula from river to river, but were left incomplete. The space occupied by this line of defenses later became Calhoun Street. The roads were sand, with brick sidewalks six feet wide in the principal streets.[6] In the 1770's Charles Town consisted of 1292 dwellings, the Exchange, two Episcopal churches, an armory, State House, one Presbyterian church, two French churches, two German churches, Congregationalist and Jewish meeting houses. A statue of William Pitt stood at the center of the intersection of Broad and Meeting streets. Facing it on the four corners were the State House, the new St. Michael's Church, the watch house and brick market house.

The greatest port between Philadelphia and the West Indies, Charles Town was the social and commercial capital of the South, a rich, proud, sophisticated and fashionable city. A weekly newspaper was established in 1732, a theater was built in 1735. In 1748 fourteen gentlemen formed a Library Society to import books and magazines from England. (By 1770 the Library Society owned Sir William Chambers's *Treatise on Civil Architecture*, 1759, James Gibbs's *Rules for Drawing*, 1732, and his *Book of Architecture*, 1728, Leoni's *Palladio*, 1716–20, and William Pain's *The Builder's Companion*, 1758.)[7] In 1762 the Saint Cecilia Society, America's oldest musical organization, was established to present concerts every ten days during winter and spring. In 1773 a Museum, located at first in rooms of the Library Society, was established to exhibit curiosities of natural science. (Alexander Garden, a Scottish-trained physician who had come to Charles Town in 1753, was a correspondent of Linnaeus and that Swedish botanist named the Gardenia after him.)[8]

Josiah Quincy, a New England minister, viewed luxury-loving Charles Town with a querulousness bred by his mixed feelings of Puritan out-

Prosperous living in 18th century Carolina, Peter Manigault and his friends at Goose Creek. Painting by George Roupell, c. 1760. *Winterthur Museum*

rage and Yankee envy: "State, magnificence and ostentation, the natural attendants of riches, are conspicuous among this people. Cards, dice, the bottle and horses engros prodigious portions of time. In grandeur, splendour of buildings, decorations, equipages, numbers, commerce, shipping and indeed in almost everything, it far surpasses all I ever saw, or ever expected to see, in America!"[9] On the eve of the Revolution, J. F. D. Smyth came to Charles Town: "The people are showy and expensive in their dress and way of living, so that everything conspires to make this the liveliest, the pleasantest and politest place, as it is one of the richest, too, in America."[10] Johann Hinrichs, a Hessian officer stationed in Charles Town during the Revolution, wrote: "No other American city can compare with Charles Town in the beauty of its houses and the splendour and taste displayed therein . . . the grandiose display of splendour, debauchery, Luxury, and extravagance."[11] Timothy Ford, a young lawyer who had moved to Charles Town from New Jersey, wrote in 1785: "In the higher classes every body must have a vast deal of waiting upon, from the oldest to the youngest. One or more servants plant themselves in the corners of the room, where they stand, and upon the slightest occasion they are called. At dinner it would seem as if the appetite were to be whetted and the victuals receive its relish in proportion to the number of attendants. They surround the table like a cohort of black guards!"[12]

Its people tied to England by birth, education and trade, Charles Town was naturally a very English city. When the Anglican Church was made the established religion of the colony in 1704, its clergy supported by public funds and serving public functions, an important institution of English culture was reaffirmed. Eliza Lucas, a girl living on her father's plantation outside Charles Town, wrote in May, 1740: "The people live very genteel and very much in the English taste."[13] In the 18th century, wealthy Charlestonians were often sent to English schools. Luxuries and books were usually imported. Governor James Glen wrote of Charles Town in 1751: "Plate begins to shine upon their sideboards, and in proportion as they thrive they delight to have good things from England."[14] In 1773 Josiah Quincy saw English gentlemen, exquisite fops affecting Continental, especially Italian, dress and manners, at the concert house in Charles Town: "We had two Macaronis present—just arrived from London. 'See the Macaroni' was common phrase in the hall."[15] In August, 1774, William Lawrence boasted that his picture frames were all "the present Taste in London."[16] From Charles Town an anonymous traveller wrote in 1774: "It is rather a Gay place, there being Public Dances, Assemblies and Plays acted in it, with horse-races about a mile off. Most people of Property keep single horse Chairs, which are very numerous indeed in the Town, but many of the Genteeler sort keep handsome four-wheeled carriages, and several carry their luxury so far as to have Carriages, Horses, Coachmen and all imported from England."[17]

Moses Lopez of Rhode Island wrote in 1764: "The City is twice as big as when I was here in the year 1742. It has increased with sumptuous brick houses in very great number. One cannot go anywhere where one does not see new buildings and large and small houses started, half finished and almost finished. To me who comes from poor humble Rhode Island it seems to me a new World!"[18] Peter Timothy, editor of the *South Carolina Gazette*, described Charles Town's rapid improvement to Benjamin Franklin in a letter of September, 1768: "Very elegant buildings are raising in almost every street by private gentlemen."[19] Timothy Ford wrote in 1785: "A small majority of the buildings are of brick tho' many are of wood. None of the dwelling houses rise higher than three stories, and by no means a majority so high, tho' a pretty good proportion of the buildings, those especially of brick, may be termed tolerably good. In some instances the projectors seem to have studied intricacy and have of course been led from uniformity."[20]

When George I ascended the throne in 1714, a wealthy Whig aristocracy came to power. These new tastemakers rejected the elaborate Baroque architecture associated with the Stuart kings in favor of a more severe style, based on the writings of the late 16th century Italian designer Andrea Palladio, known primarily through one famous work, *The Four Books of Architecture*, an illustrated guide on how to build like the Romans. The first English edition of Palladio was published by Giacomo Leoni in installments between 1716 and 1720, and Lord Burlington, the great sponsor of Palladianism in England, returned with his protegé William Kent from a trip to the Veneto of Italy where they had seen Palladio's buildings firsthand in 1719. (In 1770, Nicholas Langford on the Bay in Charles Town offered Leoni's *Palladio* for sale.)[21] English Palladianism had an inherent tendency to be stuffily bookish because that master's designs were so often copied from engravings in books. In America, where most houses were planned by their owners with the assistance of carpenters, the buildings reflected even more the character of Palladio's engraved illustrations—flat, schematic, rigidly geometric. America's mid-18th century architecture was a blend of the Baroque of the late Stuart period and Palladianism of the early Georgian period, mingled and simplified by time, distance and the colony's modest means and limited needs.

A house with temple-like pedimented portico from the most influential English edition of Palladio's *Four Books of Architecture* produced by Isaac Ware (London, 1738).

Palladio had used Roman temples as the model for many of his buildings, and the most prominent hallmark of so-called Palladian buildings was the use of columns, pediments or projecting pavilions to suggest a giant temple portico, as well as raised first floors and Venetian windows. (A Venetian, or Palladian, window is a large, round-headed window flanked by smaller rectangular windows.) Reflecting Dutch influence, roofs were more often hipped and flatter as the century progressed. (About 20% of Charles Town's houses were roofed with clay tiles from Holland.) Exterior walls were detailed in ways which emphasized horizontality—with modillion or dentil eaves cornices, moulded bricks or stone trim to decorate watertables and stringcourses. The flat, clean geometry of façades was heightened by Flemish bond brickwork with quoins at the angles, elegant glazed headers and window arches of bright red gauged brick. Sash windows were now used—with larger panes of glass as the century progressed. Fireplaces, at first framed with a simple moulded architrave, were now ever more richly decorated with shelves, supported by carved consoles, and panelled and pedimented overmantels. Fireplace walls, sometimes entire rooms from floor to ceiling, were panelled. The council chamber of Charles Town's mid-18th century State House was so elaborately panelled that it was said to appear "rather crowded and disgusting than ornamented and pleasing, by the great profusion of carved work in it."[22] In South Carolina, wide planks of cypress were the favorite material for panelling and easily-carved white pine was the favorite for applied ornamental carving. Later in the century, panelling was limited to the dado, with plain plaster or decorative wallpaper above the chair rail. (In January, 1765, John Blott, a Charles Town paperhanger, offered "a neat assortment of paper, from London, of the newest patterns. . . . The expense of papering a room does not amount to more than the cost of a middling sett of Prints.")[23] Doors were framed with pilasters or engaged columns, with cornices or pediments, whose details were usually copied from builder's guides. Stairs rose in straight flights, turned at landings, were often lit by Venetian windows, and were enclosed by heavy, carved balusters and wide handrails.

Like the best materials so often advertised as "just imported from England," Charles Town's artisans advertised themselves "just arrived from London." Thomas Newton, "Carpenter, Joiner, Cabinet & Frame maker, from London," arrived in May, 1744.[24] Patrick Mac-Lein, "Master-Bricklayer," was "just arrived from London" in May, 1748.[25] Henry Burnett, "House and Ship-Carver from London," arrived about April, 1750.[26] In May, 1751, Dudley Inman, "Carpenter and Joyner . . . from London," promised to "closely adhere to either of the orders of architecture" and give "designs of houses, according to the modern taste in building and estimates of the charge . . . buildings of all kinds, with more conveniency, strength and beauty than those commonly erected in this province."[27] John Landridge, "Carpenter and Joiner from London," advertised "neat chimney pieces and frontispieces" in August, 1759.[28] In March, 1768, Abraham Pearce, "Cabinet-Maker & Carver, from London," offered his services.[29] Though these men probably viewed themselves as mechanics rather than as creative artists, their products were often inspired.

Craftsmanship was so good and so plentiful that Charles Town exported prefabricated houses. In May, 1742, the frame of "A Dutch roof'd [gambrel] House of Two Stories, 34 by 15 Feet, with three Rooms on a Floor," its frame "ready for setting up," was offered for sale.[30] In 1767 William Logan sold "cut Frames for Houses."[31] In 1772 Martin Ramel, house carpenter, offered "A Frame of a House, two Stories high, Twenty-nine Feet Three Inches long and Seventeen Feet wide."[32] In 1764 John Knight, a merchant in Liverpool, ordered from Henry Laurens in Charles Town "the frame of a House to be Shipped."[33] When William Rigby Naylor died in October, 1773, his inventory of building materials included "a good Frame for a Wooden House 42 by 21 Feet, two Stories high, with Window Frames, separate Doors, Window Shutters and Sashes, Mouldings and Cornishes, ready made."[34]

Charles Town booksellers sold the current English architectural guides which were so necessary as models for amateur and professional builders. The typical pattern book reviewed structural methods and details of the classical orders with sample plans and elevations for houses and churches. In 1767 Robert Wells sold Colin Campbell's *Vitruvius Britannicus*, 1715–25, William Halfpenny's *The Modern Builder's Assistant*, 1757, William Pain's *The Builder's Companion*, 1758, "and other treatises on architecture." In 1769, he offered Abraham Swan's *Collection of Designs in Architecture*, 1757, *The British Architect*, 1745, and his *Carpenter's Complete Instructor*, 1768, Robert Morris's *The Modern Builder's Assistant*, 1757, and John Crunden's *Convenient and Ornamental Architecture*, 1767. In 1772, Wells had "just received from London" John Miller's edition of Palladio's *Elements of Architecture*, 1759, Isaac Ware's edition of *The First Book of Andrea Palladio's Architecture*, 1742, Matthew Darly's *The Ornamental Architect*, 1770, William Halfpenny's *The Country Gentleman's Pocket Companion*, 1753, and Robert Morris's *Architecture Improved*, 1755.[35]

Imported books, Palladianism and English culture all influenced the building of Drayton Hall on the bank of the Ashley River, twelve miles northwest of Charles Town, between 1738 and 1742.[36] Drayton Hall was built for John Drayton, the young heir of some twenty rice, indigo and cotton plantations in Carolina, Georgia and Canada. English-born Thomas Drayton, progenitor of the family in America, had come to Carolina from Barbadoes with his son—John's father—as early as 1671. When John Davis stayed at the Ashley River plantation of the brother of Charles Drayton, a later master of Drayton Hall, in 1799, he caught the spirit of the place: "I was now breathing the politest atmosphere in America. These people never moved but in a carriage, lolled on sophas instead of sitting on chairs, and were always attended by their Negroes to fan them with a peacock's feather!"[37]

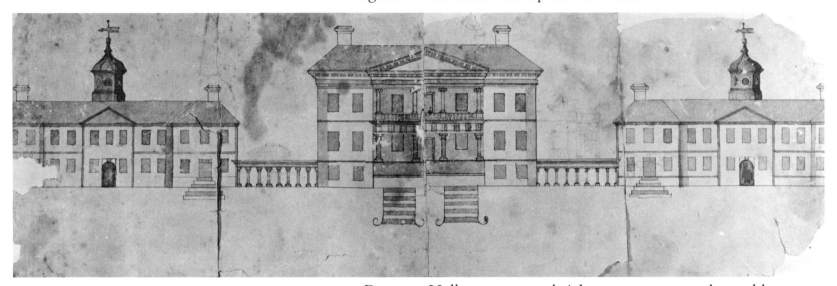

This drawing of Drayton Hall by an unidentified artist, perhaps the building's designer, shows large flankers with hipped roofs, projecting pavilions and cupolas. Instead, simpler, gable roofed flankers were built, though later destroyed. *Historic Charleston Foundation*

Drayton Hall, a two-story brick structure on an elevated basement with a double-hipped roof, has been often called the first truly Palladian house in America. The two-tiered portico on the land front appears to have been inspired by the garden façade of Palladio's Villa Pisani at Montagnana, illustrated in the second volume of his *Four Books of Architecture*. Like Palladio's original, Drayton Hall's portico faces a recessed central bay. Drayton Hall's portico is, in fact, more Palladian than English, since the open porches and loggias which were so practical in sunny Italy were not useful in the cool, wet climate of England. (This also helps explain why porticoed Palladian buildings like Drayton Hall appeared earlier and were generally more favored in the South than in the cold North.) In place of a portico, the river façade of Drayton Hall has a pediment in its roof and pediments over the three central second story windows.

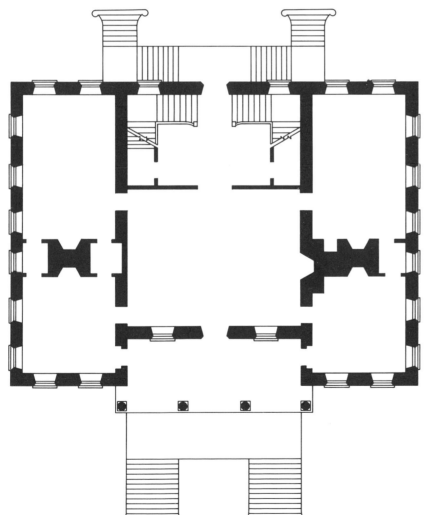

Drayton Hall, section and plan.
Section: Library of Congress

Drayton Hall, Ashley River, 1738–42, land façade

rayton Hall, river façade.

Drayton Hall, portico.

yton Hall, first story hall.

Drayton Hall, northeast chamber of the first story, with chimneypiece removed.

Drayton Hall, staircase.

Drayton Hall.
Above: Second story hall.
Below: Northeast chamber of the second story.

Two dependencies, each a two-story brick building with central chimney and gable roof, were connected to the main house by low curved walls, another Palladian device. The northern dependency was a washing, sewing and weaving house; the southern dependency was a kitchen. One dependency was destroyed in the earthquake of 1886, and the other was demolished after having been damaged in a hurricane in 1893. Other ancillary buildings included a dovecote, potato cellar, poultry house, barn, lime and brick kilns, Negro houses, rice mill and stables.

The designer of Drayton Hall is not known, but he must have come from England to supervise the construction, for its materials and execution are superb. The building's design is far ahead of anything else being done in the colonies at the time. The chimneypiece in the first story hall was copied from plate 64 of William Kent's *Designs of Inigo Jones*, which had been published in London in 1727, scarcely a decade before the building of Drayton Hall. Welsh red stone and English Portland stone were brought to America to tile the portico floor. Extra capitals and columns, shipped already carved to Carolina from England, are still stored in the basement. All the rooms of the principal stories are fully panelled with cypress. The floors are pine, the stair mahogany, the frieze, chimneypieces and pilasters are yellow poplar. Pilasters and baseboards are painted to resemble marble. The entablature of the entrance hall is enriched with triglyphs and metopes with rosettes and giant carved sunflowers.

The chimneypiece of the first story hall at Drayton Hall with its model, plate 64 of William Kent's *Designs of Inigo Jones. Kent illustration: Avery Library, Columbia University*

Drayton Hall is also notable for its extraordinary state of preservation. Spared in the Civil War, little altered during more than two centuries and for the most part untouched by well-intentioned, though sometimes heavy-handed, restorationists, Drayton Hall was owned by seven generations of the Drayton family until 1974, when it was purchased by the National Trust for Historic Preservation and the State of South Carolina. The interiors have been painted only twice, when the house was completed and again in 1870. Neither gas, water, electricity nor heating have ever been installed. The original windows, which had twelve heavily-mullioned panes in each sash, were blown out in an 1813 hurricane and replaced with larger panes and thinner mullions of the current fashion. The original slate roof was replaced with tin in the 1870's. Bricks from the tympanum of the pediment collapsed during the 1886 earthquake and were replaced with fish-scale shingles so typical of late 19th century taste.

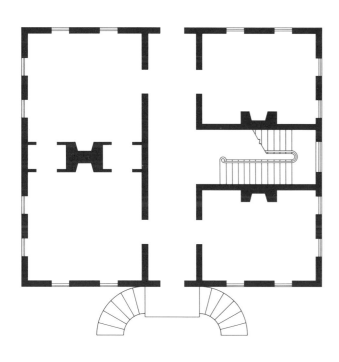

Charles Pinckney House, Charleston, 1746–47. Photograph shows ruins of the house in 1865. *National Archives*

In early 1746, Charles Pinckney, later chief justice of the province, began a new house in Charles Town, overlooking the Ashley River just north of a swampy creek which would later become Market Street. Pinckney's two-and-one-half story brick dwelling was completed in April, 1750. Stone trim was difficult to carve, expensive and therefore little used in the colonies, but Pinckney lavished carved stone on the exterior of his house, with white marble stringcourses, steps and monumental Ionic pilasters supporting a pediment with bull's-eye window. (Merchant Henry Laurens sold Pinckney imported marble mantels for the house in 1747.) The kitchen was located in a partially excavated basement, an arrangement which was unusual in the city. A pair of steps led to the front door. The interiors of the first story were fully panelled, and the hall floor was paved with stone. "Great stairs . . . with rope Twist & Brackets" led to the second story, its landing lit by a Venetian window. The grand second story drawing room had a fourteen-foot cove ceiling. In Charles Town, houses with central hall plans generally had an oversized, richly decorated chamber at the front of the second story, the urban equivalent of the English great hall moved upstairs. Pinckney's mansion must have been one of the great houses of the colonies, but it was not unique, even in Charles Town, for the owner's specifications instruct the carpenters to make the panelling of the first story parlor "as Capt. Shubrick's dining room in done," the entry to be paved "as Mr. C. Justice Whitaker's Entry is," and the second story dining room to be finished "as Mr. Greeme's is, if the charge be not too great."[38] The house was destroyed by fire in 1861.

In 1751 rapidly expanding Charles Town was divided into two parishes and a new church, St. Michael's, was to be built on the site of the original St. Philip's at the corner of Broad and Meeting streets and serve the people living in the southern parts of the city.[39] The cornerstone of St. Michael's was laid by the colonial governor in February, 1752, but construction was delayed when craftsmen and money were diverted to build a new State House diagonally across the street, and the church was not opened for services until February, 1761. The *South Carolina Gazette* reported: "This Church will be built on the Plan of one of Mr. Gibson's Designs."[40] This is believed to be a garbled reference to James Gibbs and his *Book of Architecture*, published in 1728. A building committee probably selected a plan from the book—perhaps plate 24, which resembles St. Michael's—and then left the details to a local builder, an Irishman named Samuel Cardy. Bricks for St. Michael's were made by Zachariah Villepontoux at his Parnassus Plantation on the Back River. The slate, glass, floor tile and iron came from England and Holland. The original plan for St. Michael's called for large interior columns, but by October, 1753, it was evident that the roof would stand without interior support, so these were eliminated and the foundations already laid were removed. Ceiling decorations were carved in cypress and cedar. Eight bells for the steeple were brought from England in 1764. The organ case was installed in 1768. The forty-two-light chandelier was shipped from England in 1803. In 1859, James Silk

St. Michael's Church, Meeting Street, Charleston, 1752–61. *Photograph by F. S. Lincoln: Pennsylvania State University*

Buckingham, an English traveller, called St. Michael's "a fine old structure, so exactly like the English metropolitan churches . . . that it was difficult not to imagine one's-self in London."[41]

The remarkable steeple of St. Michael's—186 feet tall, taller than the church is long—has been a landmark for mariners entering the harbor for more than 200 years. Indeed, the church's builder, Samuel Cardy, was a lighthouse builder, the edifice was paid for in part with funds intended for a lighthouse and the church may have been used as a lighthouse. George Milligen-Johnston described the steeple in 1763: "A lofty and well-proportioned Steeple . . . rises to a considerable Height. The principal Decoration of the lower Part is a handsome Portico with Doric Columns, supporting a large angular Pediment, with a Modilion Cornice. Over this rises two square Rustic Courses. In the lower one are small round Windows on the North and South; in the other, small square ones. On the East and West from this the Steeple rises octangular, having Windows on each Face, with Ionic Pilasters between each, whose Cornice supports a Balustrade. The next Course is likewise octagonal, has sashed Windows and Festoons alternately on each Face, with Pilasters and a Cornice, upon which rises a circular Range of Corinthian Pillars, with a Balustrade connecting them. . . . The Body of the Steeple is carried up octangular within the Pillars, on whose Intablature the Spire rises, and is terminated by a gilt Globe, from which rises a Vane, in the Form of a Dragon. This Steeple is . . . very useful to the Shipping, who see it long before they make any other Part of the Land."[42]

Churches of the Anglican faith continued to be important public works throughout the mid-18th century. Prince George's Church, Georgetown, was built between 1741 and 1750. Exterior walls are laid in English bond, ornamental pilasters are laid in all-header bond, and a tower, added in 1824, is laid in American bond. Inside, Tuscan columns support a barrel-vaulted ceiling. The pews and other parts of the interior were burned during the Revolution. An organ gallery was installed in 1808.

Prince William's Church, Sheldon, was built in 1753. It was burned in 1779 by a British force marching from Charles Town to Savannah. Rebuilt in 1826, the church was once again burned in 1865 by Sherman's army heading from Savannah into South Carolina. The building is still a much revered ruin, notable as an early example of a temple-form building and for the moulded brick used in the columns of the portico and in the engaged columns which surround the other three walls of the building.

St. Michael's Church, interior.

Prince William's Church, Sheldon, 1753.
Watercolor by Charles Fraser, c. 1800.
Carolina Art Association

Pompion Hill Chapel was built on the Cooper River near present-day Huger in 1763, replacing a decaying thirty-foot-square cypress structure of 1703. Zachariah Villepontoux, who had supplied the bricks for St. Michael's Church in Charles Town, made the bricks for Pompion Hill and carved his initials on the north and south doors. The church's animated exterior has a slate-covered, jerkinhead roof, arched windows and a projecting chancel with Venetian window. Inside, brick and red tile floors are laid in a herringbone pattern, the walls are white plaster and there is a cove ceiling.

St. Stephen's Church at St. Stephen's was built between 1767 and 1769.[43] The building committee received proposals for building a new church in May, 1764. In April, 1765, the committee rejected the first bricks made for the edifice by Joseph Pamor. Bricks were finally supplied by Francis Villepontoux, nephew of Zachariah. William Axon, the brickmason who had worked at Pompion Hill, also worked at St. Stephen's. In July and August, 1768, three members of the building committee resigned over a dispute about the "verry Singular" arrangement of the pews. In September, the committee hired a carpenter to erect columns and a gallery at the rear of the new church. Flemish bond walls, with brick Doric pilasters and round-headed windows, support a wide, wood cornice and tall gambrel roof with curvilinear gables.

St. James's Church, on the south side of Wambaw Creek near where it flows into the Santee River, was built in 1768 in the vicinity of McClellanville. St. James's, Santee, like the Sheldon church, has a portico with beautifully moulded brick columns. The rear portico was bricked

Pompion Hill Chapel, Huger vicinity, 1763. *Photographs by Frances Benjamin Johnston: Library of Congress*

St. Stephen's Church, St. Stephen's, 1767–
69. *Exterior photograph: Carolina Art
Association*

St. James's Church, Santee, McClellanville vicinity, 1768.

Miles Brewton House, 27 King Street, Charleston, 1765–69.

in to form a small chamber. The original seating plan was changed at an early date, with the chancel moved from beneath a Venetian window on the north wall to its present location near the center of the western wall.

Miles Brewton's house in Charles Town is often compared with Drayton Hall. Both buildings were meticulously and self-consciously designed in the latest architectural mode, sumptuously decorated and specifically Palladian in inspiration. Miles Brewton, a merchant who had made a fortune in the slave trade, began construction of his house at 27 King Street in 1765. It was completed in 1769, a two-story brick structure over an elevated basement, with a hipped roof, modillion eaves cornice and intricately carved fretwork frieze. A two-tiered portico, with Ionic and Tuscan columns, an oval window in its pediment and a stone-tiled floor, is approached by a pair of white marble steps. The Palladian impression of the portico is increased by the use of Scamozzi Ionic capitals, so called because they were illustrated by Ottavio Bertotti Scamozzi, an early popularizer of Palladio's architecture. The elliptical fanlight of the front entrance is the only one known in colonial America. The basement is laid in English bond, and the two main stories in Flemish bond. The front façade has flat arches with voussoirs of gauged brick, while the side façades have simple jack arches. On the first and second stories of the south side, jib windows open behind wrought iron railings.

Miles Brewton House, doorway of first story chamber.

The rich interior is decorated with fully panelled rooms, mahogany doors, marble mantels, elaborate overmantels, intricately carved pilasters, pediments and cornices. The hall is paved with Purbeck stone, noted for its hard texture, from the hills of Dorset. The mahogany stair, whose step-ends are adorned with rocaille scrolls, is lighted by a large Venetian window set in a projecting tower. The second story drawing room has a cove ceiling, seventeen feet high, and retains its original chandelier. The central carved panel of the marble mantel depicts a shepherd in tailcoat and cocked hat, flanked by his humble cottage and grateful flock. Josiah Quincy visited Miles Brewton's house in March, 1773: "Dined with considerable company at Miles Brewton, Esqr's, a gentleman of very large fortune, a most superb house. The grandest hall I ever beheld, azure blue stain window curtains, a rich blue paper with gilt, mashee borders, most elegant pictures, excessive grand and costly looking glasses, &c. At Mr. Brewton's side board was very magnificent plate. . . . A very fine bird kept familiarly playing over the room, under our chairs and the table, picking up the crumbs, &c., and perching on the window, side board and chairs. Vastly pretty!"[44] The finest dwelling in Charles Town, Brewton's house inevitably served as headquarters for

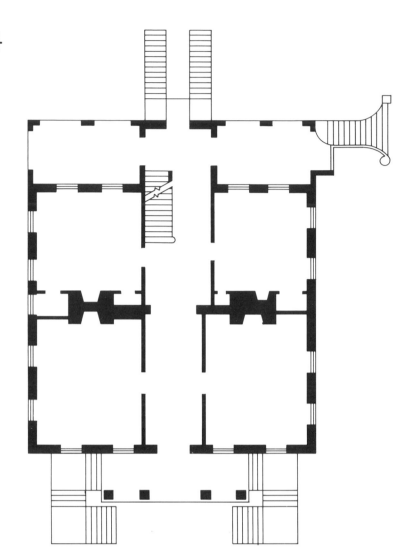

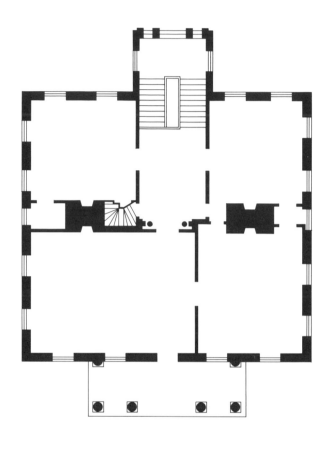

Miles Brewton House, plans of first
and second floors.

the British commander during the Revolution and for Union generals at
the close of the Civil War.

Ezra Waite, who described himself in 1769 as "Civil Architect,
House-builder in general, and Carver, from London," claimed that he
"did absolutely construct every individual part . . . and drew the same at
large for the house joiners and carpenters to work by and also conducted the execution thereof at Miles Brewton's house." He said that
twenty-seven years' experience qualified him to satisfy any gentleman
"either by plans, sections, elevations or executions."[45] When Waite
died in November, 1769, he left behind "two Negro Fellows and three
Boys, one of the fellows a Bricklayer; several pieces of curious Carved
Work, his Tools, Books, Cloaths, &c."[46] Waite needed books which
would show him how to draw plans and elevations, copy rich decora-

Miles Brewton House, view of stairhall from rear.

Miles Brewton House, second story ballroom.

Miles Brewton House, doorway in second story ballroom.

Exchange, East Bay Street, Charleston, 1767–71.
Top: View of west front with the cupola designed
by Charles Fraser in 1833, photograph before
1886. *Library of Congress.* Bottom: View of the
east front, detail from Thomas Leitch's panorama
of Charleston in 1774. *Museum of Early Southern
Decorative Arts*

tive details conceived by professional designers in England, calculate the complicated geometry of stairs and the correct proportions of the classical orders and estimate costs for his customers. Waite's library, reconstructed from a short title list made at the time of his death, is believed to have included Chippendale's *Gentleman & Cabinet-Maker's Director*, 1754, Abraham Swan's *Collection of Designs in Architecture*, 1757, Robert Morris's *Rural Architecture*, 1750, or its later revision, *Select Architecture*, 1755, Edward Oakley's *The Magazine of Architecture*, 1730, P. Baretti's *A New Book of Ornaments*, 1762, Daniel Garrett's *Designs & Estimates for Farmhouses*, 1747, Batty Langley's *The Builder's Director*, 1746, and another volume listed as "The Practical Measurer."[47]

In 1767 the provincial Assembly granted £60,000 "for the building of an Exchange and Custom House and a new watch house" in Charles Town. Construction of the new Exchange was supervised by John and Peter Horlbeck, brothers who had come from Germany to Carolina by way of England in 1764. In January, 1769, the *Gazette* reported: "Last Thursday evening arrived . . . a large quantity of Portland Stone for the new Exchange in this town, with Mr. John Horlbeck, one of the contractors for building that edifice. This is the third importation of this kind for that work."[48] In November: "In the Snow *Chatty*, arrived this week from Poole, are come about 60 Tons of Stone for our new Exchange, which is raising with great Dispatch."[49] The Exchange, its cost paid by special import duties, was completed in 1771.

Its designer was William Rigby Naylor, a draftsman and purveyor of building materials, whose plans and elevations for the Exchange have survived. (Thomas Woodin, a carver, cabinetmaker and drawing teacher who later held a position in the customs office, was also paid £36–15 for "a plan of the intended Exchange.") In October, 1772, Naylor taught "the Art of Drawing Architecture" in Charles Town.[50] When he died in the following year, Naylor's property included "Sets of surveying Instruments . . . Drawing Instruments . . . a large Chest of Carpenter's Tools . . . A Variety of Locks, Hinges, Screws, Brads, &c. . . . two handsome Marble Slabs for Hearths, Boxes of Glass . . . seven Casks of Nails."[51]

The design of the Exchange, with its rusticated ground story, Gibbs door surrounds, Venetian windows and cupola, reminds us of many provincial English public buildings of the period—and in particular of Plate 44, "Market or Town-House," in Robert Morris's *Select Architecture* of 1755. (The Gibbs surround, decorative blocks of stone around doors and windows, was named after James Gibbs, the architect who

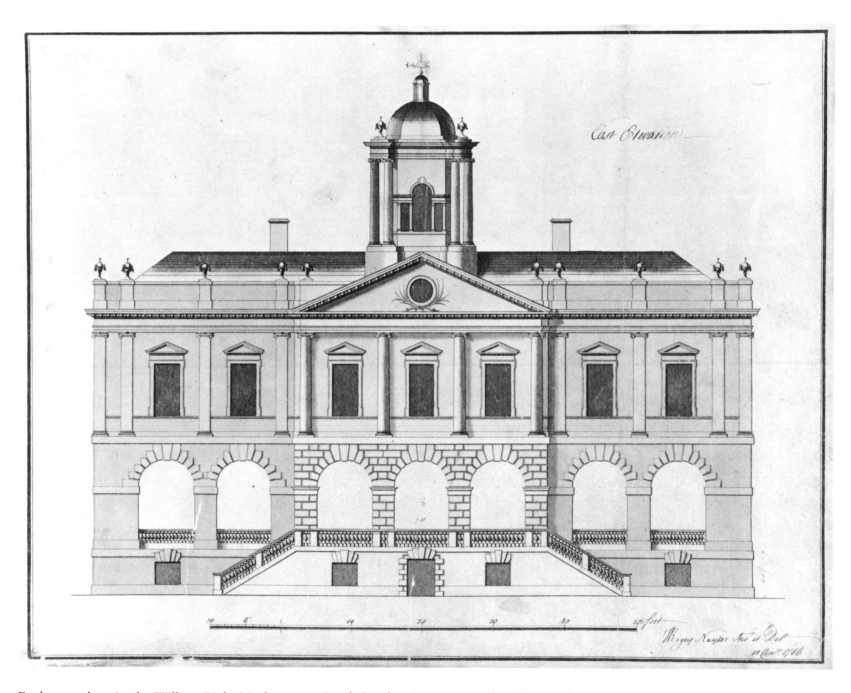

East Elevation

Rigby Naylor Inv.t et Del.t
18 Oct.r 1766

Exchange, elevation by William Rigby Naylor, 1766. *South Carolina Department of Archives and History*

Plan of a typical Charleston single house: Robert Pringle House, 70 Tradd Street, 1774, tracing of a drawing made in 1789 (porches not shown).
Charleston Museum

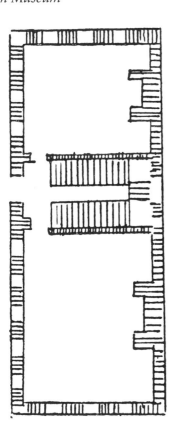

popularized it.) The Exchange's steps, handrail and balusters were Portland stone, the piazza floor was paved with Purbeck stone, and the roof was Welsh slate. The basement contained custom offices; the first story was an open arcade which served as a public market and meeting place; the second story was offices for the colonial government.[52] A so-called "Great Room" on the second story was, alas, replaced with a staircase in the 19th century. It must have been a splendid chamber, with its wainscotted walls fourteen-feet high, eight columns and twenty pilasters, pediments over the doors, a three-foot high Ionic entablature, a cove ceiling rising to at least twenty feet and two chimneypieces.

Thomas Leitch's panorama of Charles Town, painted in 1774, shows the waterfront dominated by the new Exchange, whose main façade originally faced the Cooper River. Today this eastern front has been obscured by more recent buildings erected on later landfill, and the open loggias of the principal story have been enclosed. When East Bay was widened about 1800, projecting wings on the western façade, which contained stairs, were removed. The original cupola, with its four Venetian windows and eight Ionic columns, was replaced in 1833 with another designed by Charles Fraser, Charleston lawyer-turned-artist. Fraser's cupola and the original parapet and stone urns were lost in the 1886 earthquake. The building was more or less restored to something approximating its mid-19th century appearance in 1975–81.

During the second half of the 18th century, Charles Town developed a distinctive and persistent house type.[53] This "single house"—so called at the time—was one room wide, two rooms deep, divided by a transverse stair hall, with the narrow end of the building facing the street. A public entrance on the street served a shop or office, and a family entrance led from the building's side into the stair hall. When Amarinthea Elliott signed a contract for building a house in August, 1789, it was to be "a compleat well-finished dwelling house commonly called a single house, three stories high . . . twenty-two feet wide or thereabouts and forty-six feet long or thereabouts, with two rooms on a floor and an entry leading to a stair case in or near the centre of the said house nine feet wide in the clear . . . to be built on a good brick foundation with two stacks of chimneys so as to allow one fire Place in each room."[54]

It appears that the single house did not evolve until the second half of the 18th century, for the 1739 view of Charles Town shows buildings crowded together with common walls and gable roofs whose ridges run parallel to the street. But the characteristic pre-Revolutionary single house had a hipped roof and was generally freestanding. Either the

Postmaster Bacot House, 54 Tradd Street, Charleston, mid-18th century.

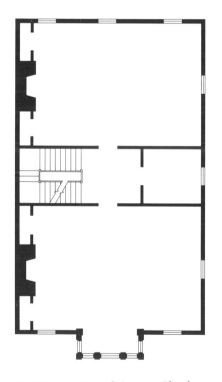

William Burroughs House, Broad Street, Charleston, 1772–74. Despite its typical plan, this single house had an elegantly detailed façade with pedimented windows and Venetian window over its Roman Doric porch.

engraver was inaccurate, or the single house was evolving out of sight behind the buildings along the waterfront, or the typical single house simply did not develop until after 1739. Detached houses with separate hipped roofs would not spread fire as quickly as houses with common walls and contiguous roofs. Perhaps the form of Charles Town dwellings was deliberately changed after the disastrous fire of 1740? Single houses persisted until the mid-19th century but with some evolution: in the later examples, gable roofs replace hipped roofs, and side porches, a customary part of the single house by the end of the 18th century, become more elaborate.

Robert Pringle's house at 70 Tradd Street, 1774, has the representative plan of a single house with especially fine decorative interior details. The mahogany stair is finished with turned balusters all the way from the first story to the fourth-floor attic. Peter Bocquet's house at 95 Broad Street, built about 1770, is another fine single house. It has been much altered but retains one superbly carved overmantel. Humphrey Sommers, a bricklayer from the west of England who worked at St. Michael's Church, built his house at 128 Tradd Street about 1765, with an unusual L-shaped plan. Front windows have pediments, pulvinated friezes and supporting brackets. The stair landing is lit by a Venetian window in a partially projecting stair tower. The William Burroughs House, built between 1772 and 1774 on Broad Street for a lawyer and judge who had come to Carolina at the age of fourteen, was demolished in 1928, but the handsome second-story drawing room, with its Venetian window, which projected over the entrance portico, was saved and installed at the Henry Francis du Pont Winterthur Museum in 1959.[55]

A fine group of important houses from the 1760's and 1770's testify to the lavish quality of building in Charles Town. These houses generally were three stories over a low foundation, most often of brick but sometimes of frame construction, with hipped roof and a projecting, pedimented central pavilion. A central hall led beneath an elliptical arch to a wider rear hall and stair, with massively carved balusters and handrail, which ascended to a landing, lit by a Venetian or round-headed window. The front rooms, often panelled on all four walls with wide cypress boards from floor to ceiling, were generally more lavishly decorated than those at the rear, which might only have panelling against the fireplace wall and plain plaster over panelled wainscot elsewhere. The most elaborate room of all was generally a large drawing room at the front of the second story. Rooms were usually finished with modillion or dentil cornices, interior shutters and window seats, and intricately carved mantels and overmantels.

William Burroughs House, views of fireplace wall and Venetian
window in front chamber of second story. *Winterthur Museum*

Humphrey Sommers House, 128 Tradd Street, Charleston,
c. 1765, chimneypiece in first story chamber.

Humphrey Sommers House, Venetian window in stairhall.

Humphrey Sommers House, chimneypiece in second story chamber.

Peter Bocquet House, 95 Broad Street, Charleston, c. 1770,
chimneypiece in second story chamber.

John Edwards House, 15 Meeting Street, Charleston, 1770. *Photograph by Frances Benjamin Johnston: Library of Congress*

Sometime after 1760 John Bull, or another member of his family, built a house at 34 Meeting Street, now generally identified by the name of a later owner, Daniel Huger. Bull, born at Ashley Hall Plantation, was a member of the provincial Assembly and militia. The façade has a projecting pavilion but has lost its pediment, which probably collapsed during the 1886 earthquake. The upstairs drawing room retains a moulded plaster ceiling and handsome overmantel, though the mantel itself has been replaced. William Branford's house at 59 Meeting Street was built sometime between 1751, when he married, and 1767, when he died. Branford was a planter in St. Andrew's Parish who travelled to his waterfront plantations on his own schooner, "Horseshoe." Branford's second story drawing room is a marvel, decorated with stop-fluted pilasters, Corinthian capitals and Greek meander as a chair rail.

John Edwards built his house at 15 Meeting Street in 1770. Its cypress façade is sawed and painted to look like stone, an effect which George Washington called "rusticated boards." The hipped roof has a modillion eaves cornice and a pediment supported by scroll brackets. The stair, with its too intricately carved balusters, is believed to date from the Colonial Revival, not the colonial, period. Daniel Heyward's house was built at 87 Church Street about 1770. It was inherited seven years later by his son, Thomas Heyward, a signer of the Declaration of Independence. About 1883, when the building became a bakery and a shop front was installed, much of the ground story was altered. Acquired by the Charleston Museum in 1929, the front portion of the hall, the left front first story chamber and lower left corner of the façade had to be reconstructed. The William Gibbes House was built at 64 South Battery between 1772 and 1779 with additions in 1794. The owner, a shipper, could see his wharfs and vessels from his front door. The marble front steps were added in the early 19th century when some interior redecorations were made in the Adam style.

Colonel John Stuart's house was built at 106 Tradd Street about 1772 for an immigrant who came from Scotland in 1743 and became a rich Indian trader and Superintendent of Indian Affairs. A Tory, he fled from Carolina to Florida in 1775 and his house was confiscated by the Revolutionary Council. The house has a sidehall plan. An intricately carved frontispiece has a pediment supported by engaged Corinthian columns, and the front windows have pediments. The cypress weatherboarding has been laid flush to give the appearance of smooth masonry. The carved cypress interiors of two principal rooms, with their fine overmantels, were removed in 1927 and installed at the Minneapolis Institute of Art in 1931.

John Edwards House, chimneypieces in first story chambers.

William Branford House, 59 Meeting Street, Charleston. Top: Second story drawing room. Bottom: Second story bedroom. View of the exterior is illustrated on page 190.

Daniel Heyward House, 87 Church Street, Charleston, c. 1770.

Daniel Heyward House, stair hall.

Daniel Heyward House, second story chamber.

84

Colonel John Stuart House, 106 Tradd Street, Charleston, c. 1772, chimneypiece of the front second story chamber. *Minneapolis Institute of Art*

William Gibbes House, 64 South Battery, Charleston, 1772–79, with additions of 1794.
Photograph by Frances Benjamin Johnston: Library of Congress

III.
Across the Frontier,
1760–1830

Oconee Station, Walhalla vicinity, 1762.

The province of Carolina in the mid-18th century was a strip of rice and indigo plantations, stretching some fifty miles deep along the rivers and swamps of the coastal low country; a sparsely settled middle country of cowherders and small farmers below the sandhills; and a near no-man's land of venturesome pioneers and Indian traders on the rolling piedmont of the back country.[1] Most of the people of Carolina—10,000 whites and 20,000 blacks in 1730—lived within fifty miles of Charles Town. Fort Moore, seven miles below Augusta, on the Savannah River, and Fort Congarees, near present-day Columbia, were built in 1716. In 1730 Governor Robert Johnson laid out townships on inland rivers of the middle country, intended to attract new settlers: Purrysburg and New Windsor on the Savannah, Williamsburg on the Black River, Orangeburg on the Edisto, Amelia on the Santee, Saxe Gotha and Fredericksburg on the Congaree, Kingston and Queensboro on the Peedee. Germans from Pennsylvania settled on the Peedee, Scotch-Irish settled on the Black River, Huguenots settled on Long Cane Creek at the town of New Bordeaux. About 1762 Colonel Archibald Montgomery, leader of expeditions against the Cherokee Indians, built Oconee Station, a stone blockhouse with walls two feet thick on a still remote hillside near present-day Walhalla. But significant settlement of the back country was delayed until the end of Indian wars in the 1760's. By 1760, 19,000 whites and 53,000 blacks lived on the coast, 9000 whites and 1500 blacks lived in the middle country, and 700 whites and 500 blacks lived in the back country.

Charles Woodmason, a stiff Anglican minister who preached in the Carolina back country between 1766 and 1773, wrote: "The people . . . new settlers, extremely poor . . . live in log cabins like hogs . . . a mix'd medley from all countries and the off-scouring of America. . . . Behold on ev'ry one of these rivers, what number of idle, profligate, audacious vagabonds! Lewd, impudent, abandon'd prostitutes, gamblers, gamesters of all sorts—horse thieves, cattle stealers, hog stealers, hunters going naked as Indians, women hardly more so!"[2] The settlers of the back country raised corn, peas, beans, pumpkins, rye, potatoes, turnips, peaches, pears and apples, and lived off a diet of corn meal, wheat flour, salt beef and pork. They wore leather shirts, leggins and moccasins. The men tied up their long hair in a little deerskin bag or rolled it up in a ribbon or bear's gut. Their chief amusements, as listed in 1826, were: "wrestling, jumping, running foot races, fiddling, dancing, shooting, playing blind man's bluff, snuggle the brogue, rimming the thimble, selling of pawns, crib and tailor, grinding the bottle, brother I am bob'd, black bear, dropping the glove, swimming and diving."[3] It might take a week for a horseman to ride from Camden to Charles Town, perhaps a week or two longer for a wagon to make the same trip. The only formal institutions of this rough, restless country were militia companies, local justices of the peace and churches. The commander of Fort Moore described the backwoodsmen of the mid-18th century as "little more than white Indians." This was a land of religious dissenters, small farmers and democrats, separated by more than distance from the Anglican, plantation-dominated, aristocratic coast. In 1821, the Episcopal bishop of Charleston called the backwoods of South Carolina "the fog end of creation."[4]

This crude but potentially powerful back country remained poor until the coming of cotton at the end of the 18th century and isolated until the coming of the railroads early in the 19th century. La Rochefoucauld-Liancourt wrote in 1799: "All South Carolina contains scarcely five or six villages, if four or five compact houses deserve this name."[5] Until at least the late 1820's, the interior of South Carolina remained a great forest punctuated by occasional farms and some twenty district villages located on interior waterways. Camden, on the east bank of the Wateree River, was a town of 300 houses, 2000 inhabitants and considerable trade with the back country. Cheraw, on the west side of the Peedee River, where steamboats loaded for trips to Charleston

"South East View of Greenville, South Carolina," drawing by Joshua Tucker, 1825. The porticoed brick courthouse was designed by Robert Mills in 1821. *Abby Aldrich Rockefeller Folk Art Center, Williamsburg*

and Georgetown, had 150 houses and 1300 people. Georgetown, a busy rice port on the north side of the Sampit River, had some 300 houses and 600–700 whites. Barnwell had 120 people, thirty houses, a courthouse, jail and female academy. Society Hill, whose houses were "so scattered that, as you ramble, you come upon them unawares," was a village of 120 people, thirty-five houses, six stores, two taverns, a tanyard, two blacksmiths. Chesterfield had one hundred people, twelve houses, two stores and a brick courthouse. Conwayborough had one hundred citizens and twenty-five houses. Marion had one hundred inhabitants, thirty houses, a new brick courthouse, jail and academy. Orangeburg near the Edisto River, had a population of 150 people, including five merchants, three lawyers, two physicians, two coach-makers, a tailor, blacksmith and tavernkeeper. Winnsborough, between the Broad and Wateree rivers, had fifty houses and eight or ten stores, most of them along one big street. Pendleton, near Eighteen Mile Creek, was a village of forty houses, two churches, a courthouse, jail, academy and newspaper office. Laurens on the Little River had 250 inhabitants and thirty-five houses. Lancasterville had 260 inhabitants, thirty houses, a store, courthouse, jail and brick academy. Greenville had 500 whites and seventy houses. Abbeville was a pleasant village of 400 people, forty houses, a courthouse, jail, arsenal and magazine.[6]

The log cabin was the ubiquitous dwelling of the 18th and 19th century American frontier. Colonial timber frame construction used square logs, fitted together in a complicated pattern with wooden pegs. The log cabin was made by laying round logs horizontally, fitting them together at the corners with notched joints, each log held in place by the weight of the log above it. Room sizes were limited by the length of straight tree trunks which did not taper too much. The true log cabin, unknown to the early colonists or the American Indians, was brought to the Delaware Valley by Swedish settlers in the mid-17th century.

Sometime between 1798 and 1806, C. W. Jansen wrote of Carolina frontiersmen's huts: "They are constructed of pine trees, cut in lengths of ten or fifteen feet, and piled up in a square, without any other workmanship than a notch at the end of each log to keep them in contact. When this barbarous pile is raised between six and seven feet, they split the remainder of their logs to the thickness of two or three inches and, by laying them over the whole in a sloping direction, form the roof. . . . The summer's scorching sun and the bleek winds of winter are equally accessible to this miserable dwelling."[7] In 1802 John Drayton wrote: "The houses of the poorest sort of people are made of logs, let into each other at the ends, their interstices being filled up with moss, straw or

A frontiersman's cabin, drawn by Frederick Law Olmsted in 1854. *University of Georgia Libraries*

clay; and are covered with clapboards. Their plans are simple, as they consist only of one or two rooms; and the manners of the tenants are equally plain."[8] In 1804 Robert Mills wrote in a letter that the dwellings of Carolina's interior were "mostly built of logs plaster'd with clay."[9]

Andre Guillebeau, a Huguenot carpenter and small farmer, came to Carolina in 1764.[10] He or his descendants built a small log house in McCormick County sometime in the late 18th or early 19th century. The original house was a two-story structure with a gable roof, twenty-six feet wide and seventeen feet deep, with exterior brick chimney. Its log foundation rested directly on hard clay, with a rectangular shallow cellar dug into the ground. The window sashes now in place, though modern, probably represent enlargements of earlier window openings. The present stair is new. Originally there would have been a ladder leading to the second story.

Benjamin Busey is believed to have begun construction of a log house of a different type just south of Woodruff between 1787, when he received his grant, and 1790, when he sold his land.[11] Busey's original house, a single log room, was enlarged in the early 19th century by the addition of another log room, completely separate from the original cabin but sharing the same chimney. The two structures were held up by the old chimney between them, much like two saddlebags suspended over a horse's back. Thus, structures of this type are often called saddlebag cabins. The early construction date of the original cabin is indicated by the lack of window glass, batten shutters, segmental arched fireplace opening and dovetail log jointing.

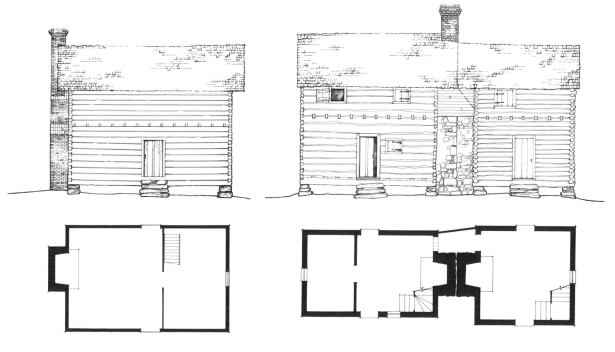

Left: Andrew Guillebeau Cabin, McCormick County, late 18th century. Right: Benjamin Busey Cabin, Woodruff vicinity, c. 1787–90. *Elevations and plans by Martin Meek for The Beehive Press*

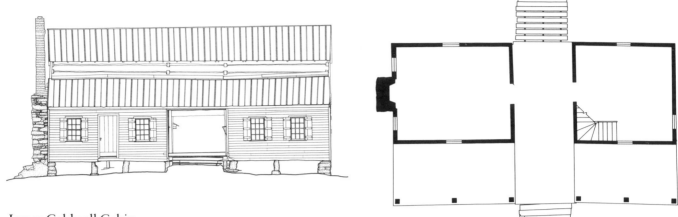

James Caldwell Cabin,
Abbeville County, c.
1800. *Elevation:
Library of Congress*

About 1800, James Caldwell built a substantially larger cabin of a third type approximately two miles east of the Savannah River in the vicinity of present-day Lowndesville.[12] Its original two rooms were connected by a wide, open passageway, which served as sitting and dining room in warm weather. This open hall also served as a kennel for the family dog, giving to this house type the delightful soubriquet of dogtrot cabin. Originally a one-story log house, one room deep, resting on fieldstone piers, Caldwell's cabin was enlarged with extra room and frame additions at the front and rear, and about 1850 the roof was raised by the addition of three logs to make second-story rooms. Today a visitor to Caldwell's cabin would find an old couple living much the same isolated, primitive life that the original builder must have spent in the Carolina forest 180 years ago, with a bucket of well water and dipper on the kitchen table and a fire for heat and light smoldering in the living room chimney. Another large surviving dogtrot cabin was built about 1780 three miles southeast of Saluda by James Bonham, a Revolutionary soldier from Maryland.

A traveller of 1825 reported: "The habitations of the common people are constructed of logs, and one story high. The chimneys are of the same material, but plastered with clay to prevent their taking fire. . . . The houses are generally about twelve feet wide by twenty-four in length. A partition in the middle divides them into two rooms. One . . . is used as a bedroom for the heads of the family, the other is occupied as a sitting, drawing & dining room. The furniture of this is composed of about a dozen strong oaken chairs with seats of deer or alligator skins. . . . In addition to these, they have two shed rooms for the accommodation of visitors and children."[13] Frederick Law Olmsted wrote in 1854: "The large majority of the dwelling houses were of logs, and even those of white people were often without glass windows. . . . The whole cabin is often elevated on four corner-posts, two or three feet from the ground, so that the air may circulate under it. The fireplace is built at the end of the house, of sticks and clay, and the chimney is carried up the outside, and often detached from the log-walls. . . . The logs are usually hewn but little, and, of course, as they are laid up, there will be wide interstices between them. . . . Through the chinks, as you pass along the road, you may often see all that is going on in the house, and, at night, the light of the fire shines brightly on all sides."[14]

Walnut Grove, near Roebuck, is believed to have been built about 1765 for Charles Moore, a farmer and later schoolmaster who came from Pennsylvania in 1762. Spartanburg County was first settled in the 1750's and 1760's by settlers from Virginia, North Carolina and Pennsylvania. Its original log construction is hidden by weatherboarding, and the L-shaped front porch is a replica of one which probably dates from the second quarter of the 19th century. Interior walls and ceilings are sheathed with flush boards above panelled dado. Chimney breasts, with their wide segmental hearths so typical of the late 18th century Southern frontier, are decorated with tiers of small rectangular panels.

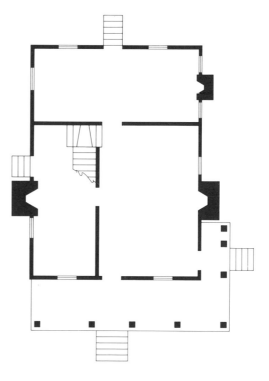

Walnut Grove, Roebuck vicinity, c. 1765, porch later.

Walnut Grove, views of
first story chambers.

Thomas Price came to the nearby neighborhood of present-day Switzer about 1790. Some four years later he purchased land near the fork of the South Tyger River and Ferguson Creek and built a truly exceptional three-story brick house.[15] Its Flemish bond walls and gambrel roof, characteristic of Delaware, Maryland and eastern Pennsylvania, suggest that Price may have come to Carolina from one of those states. The interior walls are finished with an inch-thick coat of clay and lime, mixed with hair and flax. Just to the east of the main house, a brick kitchen was also built. Until his death in April, 1820, Price operated a store, public house and post office. After the death of his widow in 1821, new owners added a wing to the west end and a servants' quarters at the rear, connected to the house by a breezeway. Both the original kitchen to the east and the later western wings have disappeared.

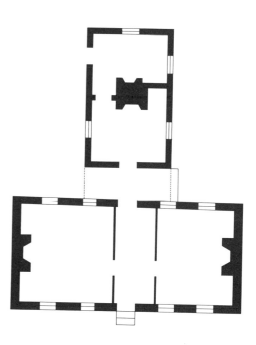

Thomas Price House, Switzer, c. 1790.

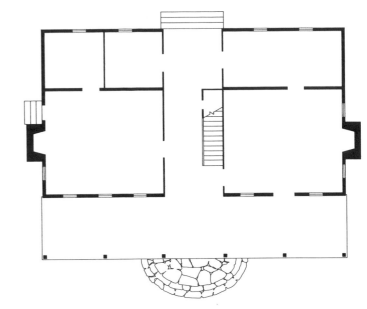

Varennes Tavern, Anderson, date uncertain.
Elevation: Library of Congress

John Norris, whose father had come to Carolina from England by way of Virginia in 1756, or his son, Jesse Ward Norris, built Varennes Tavern, five miles east of Anderson, in the late 18th or early 19th century. Alas, the house burned in 1982, but we have photographs and drawings. Though it was an old-fashioned dogtrot with an open passageway between two rooms, Varennes Tavern was of timber frame construction, not logs, and thus an important transitional dwelling, leading from primitive pioneer cabins to the comfortable farm houses characteristic of the 19th century Southern piedmont. A type often called plantation plain-style, these vernacular houses were two-story frame structures, with exterior end chimneys, central halls, gable roofs, shed rooms at the rear and sometime another shed room under part of the front porch. Chimneys of these dwellings might be decorated with diapering, cheerful patterns of colored brick set into the fabric of the wall as it was laid by the mason. An abandoned farmhouse at Sedalia, probably dating from the first quarter of the 19th century, has a chimney of this type. Interiors might be embellished with fanciful echoes of styles seen in coastal towns. McMakin's Tavern, outside Lyman, is a plantation plain-style house, built about 1800. The anonymous carpenter treated the mantel, overmantel and adjacent windows as a single architectural unit, linked by boldly carved decorations. Mountain Shoals Plantation at Enoree, built by Daniel McKee about 1820, is an elegant example of a plantation plain-style house with granite steps, three-part windows and beautifully detailed porch.

Mountain Shoals Plantation, Enoree, c. 1818–23.

McMakin's Tavern, Lyman, c. 1800,
two chambers of first story.

In 1786 Columbia, a new town at Friday's Ferry on the Congaree River, was designated the new state capital. The legislature first convened there in January, 1790. Andre Michaux, a French botanist who had come to America on an official mission to study trees which might be transplanted to Europe, described Columbia in 1802: "The number of its houses does not exceed 200; they are almost all built of wood, and painted grey & yellow, and although there are very few of them more than two stories high, they have a very respectable appearance."[16] It has been suggested, without evidence, that the Irish architect James Hoban (c. 1756–1821) might have designed the first State House at Columbia. Hoban had come to Philadelphia by 1785 and reached Charleston by May, 1790, when he offered "an evening school, for the instruction of young men in architecture."[17] The State House was a frame structure on a low brick foundation with pedimented portico and shingle roof painted brown. Like Hoban's design for the President's House at Washington, the State House at Columbia looked like an old-fashioned Palladian country house. When George Washington visited there in May, 1791, he reported that the Capitol was "a large and commodious building, but unfinished."[18] In 1805 Edward Hooker described it: "So low as to be entirely void of anything like just proportion. . . . The lower story is appropriated to the Treasurer's, Secretary's and Surveyor General's offices. There are several other rooms . . . used for little else than lodging rooms for the goats that run loose about the streets, and which, as the doors are never shut, have at all times full access."[19] The State House was moved to temporary foundations in 1853, when construction of a new Capitol was begun. The building was burned by Union troops in February, 1865.

State House, Columbia, c. 1790. Drawing by John Drayton, c. 1800. *Charleston Library Society*

IV.
The Federal Era,
1780–1830

East Battery, Charleston, 1831. Painting by S. Barnard. The second house from the left, with a fanlight door and one-story piazza, is the Charles Edmonston House of 1829 before alterations made after 1837. *The Mabel Brady Garvan Collection, Yale University Art Gallery*

In the 1790's, Charleston was only three-quarters of a mile wide and one-and-one-quarter of a mile long, stretching across the peninsula between the Ashley and Cooper rivers. In 1792 the city was still surrounded by its revolutionary fortifications. Hurricanes flooded the town, and in 1797 and 1798 the sea walls along East Bay were strengthened with palmetto baskets filled with stones, but these were blown away by storms in September, 1804. Michaux wrote of Charleston in 1802: "Two-thirds of the houses are built of wood, the rest with brick."[1] Footwalks at the sides of the dirt streets were laid with brick or stone. Sometimes a bridge of stones might help passersby get across the muddy thoroughfares. In 1817 only two streets were paved and those "only a small distance." By 1826, nearly all of East Bay and the lower parts of Broad, Tradd and Queen streets had been paved with ballast stones. Ship chandlers, the auction houses, the factors, the cotton and rice traders were all located along the bay and river. By 1830, Charleston had some 30,000 people and some 5000 buildings. In 1826 there were some two hundred house carpenters and sixty painters in South Carolina.[2] An 1831 Charleston city directory listed thirty-two carpenters, plus nine "free persons of color" who were carpenters.

In the 18th century, the modern world rediscovered the ancients. The everyday life of first century Romans was revealed by excavations which began at Herculanaeum in 1735 and at Pompeii in 1755. Robert Wood and James Dawkins described Roman antiquities of the Syrian desert in their publications, *The Ruins of Palmyra*, 1753, and *The Ruins of Balbec*, 1757. When Richard Baker, who lived on the Ashley River of South Carolina, died in 1783, his possessions included "Sixteen Views of Rome, Balbec & Palmyra."[3] Such archaeological discoveries, published in sumptuous illustrated folios, became models for a new kind of classical architecture in the last third of the 18th century. This neoclassical style took its name from the Scottish architect and designer Robert Adam, who once described himself as "antique-mad." Born in Edinburgh in 1728, Adam was the second son of Scotland's most important architect. In 1758, after four years' study in Italy, Adam, with his brothers James and William, established an architectural firm in London. In 1764 he published a book of his own about late Roman ruins located in what is now Yugoslavia, *The Ruins of the Palace of the Emperor Diocletian at Spalatro*.

Instead of the Renaissance's generalized, monumental forms, copied mostly from ancient public buildings, designers could now imitate specific, cozy details of private dwellings. Adam complained that the old Palladian buildings were "ponderous," while real Roman design was "all delicacy, gaiety, grace." In place of Palladianism's cool, impersonal, solemn, splendid grandeur, Adam's neoclassicism was cheerful, personal, vivacious, intimate. Adam's architectural practice—and his style—was concerned primarily with interior decoration. Rooms, which had earlier been almost uniformly rectangular, were now given a variety of shapes to reflect their various uses, with vaults, niches, oval or round ends and columnar screens—all inspired by late Roman planning. Adam filled his rooms with intricate decoration—anthemia, rinceaux, urns, garlands, medallions, paterae—and often highlighted them with bright, light paint colors. Mouldings and cornices were flattened, proportions lengthened. Where Palladian architecture had been monumental, masculine, muscular, this neoclassicism was intimate, feminine, graceful.

In England, Adam's fame reached its peak in the 1770's, but the style associated with his name did not cross the Atlantic until after the Revolution. He died in 1792, but his influence continued to dominate the American architectural scene for thirty more years. It simply took time for tastemakers to write and publish the books which would spread this new style. William Pain was one of the most successful popularizers of Adam architecture for carpenters and housewrights. *The Practical Builder*, originally published in London in 1774, was not issued in America until 1792; *The Practical House Carpenter* of 1784 was not printed in America until 1796; and his *Carpenter's Pocket Directory* of 1781 did not appear in America until 1797.

Adam's neoclassicism, simplified as it crossed the ocean, became what is now called in America the Federal style. Proportions of buildings, rooms, doors, cornices, mouldings and baseboards became even thinner, lighter, more delicate, because they were so often copied from engravings in books. Instead of the high hipped roofs and deep eaves so characteristic of mid-Georgian buildings, roofs were now flatter and crowned with balustrades, which obscured the roof. Circular motifs were favored—oval or round-ended rooms, round-headed windows set into recessed relieving arches and cascading spiral stairs. Swirling patterns of surface decoration on doors and window frames and mantels were executed in cast plaster or carved wood. In August, 1801, Benjamin Leefe of Charleston offered for sale "Elegant Composition Ornaments . . . for ornamenting of Chimneys, Windows, Doors &c. put up in handy packages."[4] In December, 1803, David Lopez offered "a quantity of elegant and rich Composition Work, in boxes, for rooms complete."[5] Windows and windowpanes were larger, while muntins were thinner. Doorways had semicircular or elliptical fanlights with sidelights, each composed of elaborate, intricately designed panes of glass. Marble mantels were decorated with a frieze of carved classical figures, while wood mantels were embellished with plaster ornaments cast in the form of garlands or carved sunbursts or geometric designs. Instead of the heavy panelling associated with mid-18th century taste, walls were now plastered above a simple chair rail, sometimes with wallpapers.

But these new decorative ideas did not blossom in South Carolina immediately after the Revolution. In the introduction to his *American Builder's Companion* of 1806, Asher Benjamin wrote: "Old-fashioned workmen, who have for many years followed the footsteps of Palladio and Langley, will no doubt leave their old path with great reluctance." Artisans like John Parkinson, a Charleston carver who had been apprenticed to John Lord in the 1770's, continued their old ways after the Revolution. Reliance on books of the Georgian tradition also contributed to this architectural conservatism. The Beth Elohim Synagogue, built for a Jewish congregation of Charleston established in 1749, was an old-fashioned design, loosely modeled on St. Michael's and the churches of James Gibbs of a half century earlier. The cornerstone was

Adamesque decorations in city and country.
Above: John Mark Verdier House, Beaufort, 1786.
Below: Camp Hill, Glenn Springs, 1835.

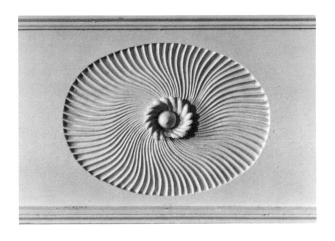

laid in September, 1792, the new synagogue was consecrated in September, 1794, and it burned in April, 1838.[6]

The arrival of the Federal style in South Carolina is associated with Charleston's Gabriel Manigault (1758–1809), rice planter, powerful Federalist and accomplished amateur architect. His great-grandfather Pierre had come from France to Carolina at the end of the 17th century. His grandfather Gabriel was a rice and indigo planter who, by the time of his death in 1781, had become the wealthiest merchant of the province. The grandson Gabriel had begun the study of law in London on the eve of the Revolution and, according to tradition, returned from his studies with a large architecture library. We know for certain that Gabriel Manigault travelled to New England, where in September, 1793, he dined with another famous amateur architect, Charles Bulfinch, in Boston. It is believed that Manigault designed at least three houses and three public buildings before moving to Pennsylvania about 1804, where he died in 1809.

In 1800, construction of a branch of the Bank of the United States was begun at the northeast corner of Broad and Meeting streets on the site of the old meat market which had burned in June, 1796. The *City Gazette* of November 8, 1800, spoke of "Messrs. M'Grath and Nicholson, the architects," but it is believed they were the builders and that Gabriel Manigault was the designer.[7] The cornerstone was laid in November, 1800, and the building was completed the following year. The Bank's hipped roof is obscured by a panelled balustrade. The lively façade includes a three-bay central pedimented pavilion with engaged Composite and Ionic columns, end bays with pilasters and quoins, windows recessed under arches and an enriched stringcourse. The entrance is finished with a coved arch decorated with swags and Tudor roses. The façade is now stuccoed, but its original appearance must have been striking, the bright red brick of the walls, laid in Flemish bond, contrasting boldly with the white marble ornamentation.

The original interior must also have been impressive.[8] Visitors entered a two-story banking room, which extended across the front of the building, overlooked by a gallery at the second story. Behind this hall were offices in the northeast and northwest corners and a grand spiral stair between them. The building continued to serve as the United States Bank until 1811, when Congress failed to renew its charter. A private commercial bank occupied the building until 1818, when it became the city hall. The interior was altered by Charles F. Reichardt in 1839. In 1882, the exterior was stuccoed, windows reglazed, parapet wall raised above the eaves and the interior rebuilt a second time.

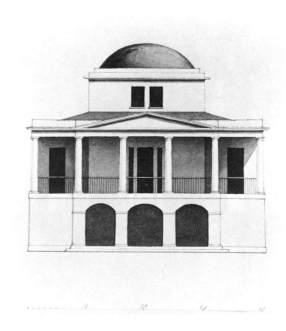

Drawing of a domed Palladian villa, possibly by Gabriel Manigault. *Private Collection*

Above: United States Bank, Broad Street, Charleston, 1800–01. Below: Orphan House Chapel, Vanderhorst Street, Charleston, 1801–02. *Library of Congress*

Sometime before 1802, Gabriel Manigault designed his own residence, now demolished, on Meeting Street, a cypress building with double-tiered porches and fluted Composite and Ionic columns. In August, 1801, construction of an Orphan House Chapel at 13 Vanderhorst Street was commenced to Manigault's design. It was completed in September, 1802, a hip-roofed brick building, finished with stucco. Four engaged Tuscan columns supported a central pedimented pavilion. It was demolished about 1954. The South Carolina Society, a charitable organization founded in 1737, completed a new hall designed by Manigault at 72 Meeting Street in 1802. The first story served as school rooms, and the second story, with delicately decorated musicians' gallery, was a meeting hall. A portico, designed by Frederick Wesner, was added in 1825.

About 1803 Gabriel Manigault designed a house for his brother Joseph at 350 Meeting Street. Visitors enter the property through a lodge with bell-shaped roof, evidently an imitation of 18th century English garden temples. The house is a three-story brick structure, laid in Flemish bond, with a hipped slate roof and two-tiered wooden porches. The second story hall is lit by a "thermal" or Diocletian window. (Popular in the Federal period, it was so called because it was modeled on the Baths, or thermae, of Diocletian.) A spiral stair is set in a round projection on the north side, and a semicircular porch on the west end balances a round-ended dining room on the east end. The house has been owned by the Charleston Museum since 1933.

Joseph Manigault House. Below: Drawing by Charlotte Drayton Manigault, c. 1830. *Private Collection.* Left: Plan.

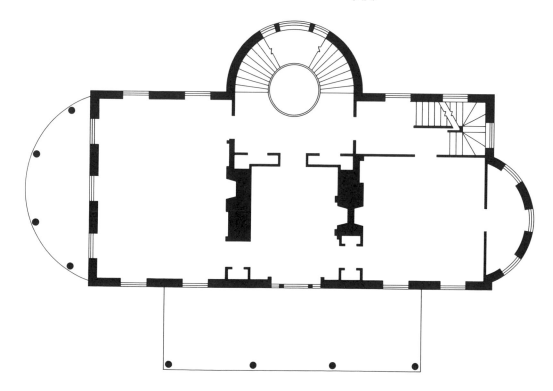

Joseph Manigault House, 350 Meeting Street, Charleston, c. 1803.

Joseph Manigault House, view of stair.

South Carolina Society Hall, 72 Meeting Street, Charleston, 1802, bandstand in the ballroom.

Like Gabriel Manigault, Henry Izard (1771–1826) was an accomplished amateur architect. Like the Manigaults, the Izards were another of those great Carolina families who had come to the colony in the late 17th century and prospered as rice and indigo planters. Henry Izard's grandfather had come from England to Carolina in 1682. His mother was a daughter of the first Royal governor of the province. Accomplished as well as privileged, these families divided their time between remote plantations in the Carolina low country, comfortable houses in Charleston and the fashionable homes of friends and relations in Philadelphia and foreign capitals, often carrying with them a pencil, brush and sketchbook. Like Gabriel Manigault, who had lived in England for a time, Henry Izard toured Europe and lived with his family in Paris in the early 1770's. In May, 1785, these parallel lives drew closer when Henry's sister Margaret married Gabriel Manigault.

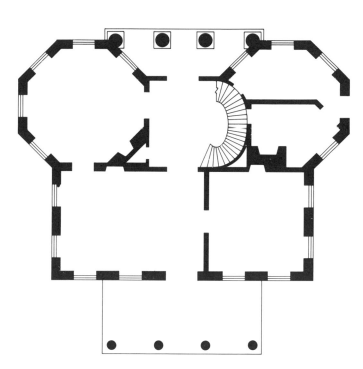

The Elms, Goose Creek, 1809. Drawing by Thomas Middleton, 1817. *Private Collection*

After his father's death in 1804, Henry Izard became proprietor of The Elms, the family plantation at Goose Creek.[9] When the old house burned in 1807, Henry replaced it with a new one of his own design. A two-story brick structure, laid in Flemish bond, with a semicircular fanlight entrance, a monumental Tuscan portico on the north side and a one-story pedimented portico on the south side, the house had a highly unusual plan, which combined the traditional great hall of colonial

The Elms, the ruins sometime after the 1886
earthquake. *Carolina Art Association*

Carolina with the octagonal rooms favored at this time by Thomas Jefferson. The plan of The Elms, 1809, certainly recalls Farmington, a house enlarged with an elongated octagon and Doric portico by Jefferson at Charlottesville, Virginia, in 1802. It is noteworthy that Henry's father had corresponded with Jefferson throughout the 1780's on agricultural matters. Asked by Izard how to educate one of his sons to be an "engineer," Jefferson replied in July, 1788, that the boy should be sent to Europe once he had reached the age of fifteen and enclosed a catalogue of a European architectural school.[10]

In December, 1818, Abiel Abbot, a minister from Andover, Massachusetts, visited The Elms: "We arrived about sunsetting on the frontier of Mr. Izard's plantation. . . . A good half mile from the mansion we descried the magnificent building. . . . The mansion fronts south & consists of a parallelogram & projections with a one-story piazza South & a two-story piazza North. The Southern piazza resembles the portico of my church; the Northern is a beautiful recess, leading into a spacious entry connected with the principal apartments. The pillars are of the Doric order & surrounded with a neat pediment. . . . From the Southern piazza you enter a hall 30 by 20 feet in the clear, which immediately communicates with the library, 20 by 20. This delightful apartment with some thousands of admirably selected books is assigned to the stranger [as a bedroom]. . . . The projection of the N.W. corner forms a superb octagonal drawing room, 24 feet diameter. A large fire place with elegant marble garniture [chimneypiece] occupies an eighth part, connected with the Hall chimney. The whole room is extremely beautiful & furnished & lighted in a tasteful manner. The musical instruments were sure to attract my attention . . . the piano . . . the guitar . . . the lyre . . . the most superb Harp I presume in Christendom. . . . We were soon introduced to the hall & partook of a plentiful repast of tea, hominy, John Cake, & meats."[11] Notably, the Izards used their great hall in 19th century Carolina as it had been used in medieval England, an an all-purpose living and dining room. The house burned about 1835. Today only the foundations of this interesting and highly original house remain.

Henry Izard also owned a farm on the Catawba River of Lancaster County. On March 16, 1812, Margaret Izard Manigault wrote to her sister Alice Izard: "My brother Henry . . . has some very original notions . . . about building. On the Catawba he says that he will have a Wigwam, Circular, & the stack of chimneys in the middle. It is to be built of Cob. It appears to me rather too fantastical—but I dare say that it would be neither ugly nor inconvenient. . . . To hear him, one would

Henry Izard's "Wigwam," drawing by Margaret Manigault, 1812. *South Caroliniana Library, University of South Carolina*

suppose that there was nothing so easy as to build a house & furnish it. . . . It will take eight days travelling from The Elms to their Wigwam!"[12] By "Cob," Margaret Manigault probably meant a concretelike mixture of clay, gravel and straw. Henry's "rather too fantastical" dwelling may not have been built, but Robert Mills marked a residence of "H. Izard" on a map in 1825 and wrote in 1826 that Izard was experimenting with vineculture at his "beautiful farm on the Catawba River."

In June, 1813, Anne Izard Deas (1779–1863), another of Henry's sisters, sent Margaret Manigault a sketch of a country house, designed by her or her brother, to be located at the "Pinewoods," one of those summer settlements to which low-country planters moved during the sickly season. She wrote, "Don't you think that is a famous house for the Woods? When it is quite finished I assure you it will be very comfortable & it looks quite pretty. It has the appearance of a Green house."[13] The Manigaults and the Izards illustrate how, in the absence of professionally trained architects, most houses were planned by their owners, with the assistance of joiners and housewrights. In most cases, the owner supplied an idea for the building's plan, giving the builder a sketch of his own devising, or taking the design from a book or pointing to another building in the neighborhood as a model. The owner generally supplied the bricks and lumber, purchasing them or having his own laborers make them. The builder was usually a carpenter or mason, but he could hire plasterers, painters or carvers to finish the interior.

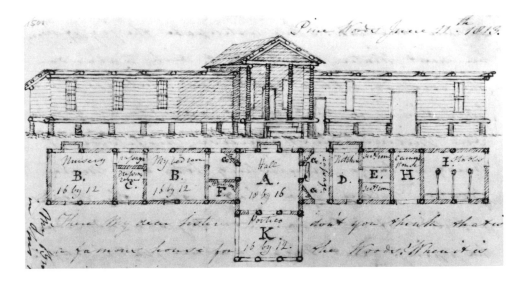

House for the Pinewoods, drawing by Anne Izard Deas, 1813. *South Caroliniana Library, University of South Carolina*

In Charleston, Arnoldous Vanderhorst, who had been Governor of South Carolina between 1792 and 1794, built a row of three houses at 78 East Bay in 1800.[14] This building, and another called North Vander-

Arnoldous Vanderhorst Row, 78 East Bay Street, Charleston, 1800. Early photograph shows the building before restoration and growth of trees which now hide the façade. *South Caroliniana Library, University of South Carolina*

horst Row, which was demolished during the Civil War, stood on either side of Vanderhorst's wharf on the Cooper River. The surviving row contains three dwellings, with separate kitchens, baths and servants' quarters in the rear. A pedimented pavilion, projecting from the center of its long façade, is emphasized by special decorations: a central Venetian window, marble lintels and ribbed and chanelled kcystones, marble quoins at the angles, and stone plaques between the second and third story windows which proudly proclaim "Vanderhorst Row 1800."

William Blacklock's house at 18 Bull Steet was built in 1800, a three-story brick structure with hipped roof and conventional central hall plan. The delicate refinement of its façade reminds us immediately of Vanderhorst Row. A central pavilion has a fanlight window in its pediment, a three-part window on the second story, a graceful, elliptical fanlight over the front door, first floor windows recessed under semi-circular relieving arches, and marble impost stripes. Elsewhere, there are keystones over windows, plaques between outer windows of the first and second stories. The finest feature of the interior is the stairhall ceiling, with its parachute-like half dome. The walls are plain plaster over panelled dado, with interior shutters throughout. Otherwise, the interior has been much changed.

William Blacklock House, 18 Bull Street, Charleston, 1800. *Photograph by F. S. Lincoln: Pennsylvania State University*

An immense and stylish house at 14 George Street was begun by Frances Middleton in 1797 and completed by her new husband Thomas Pinckney in 1801. Four stories tall, with great oval rooms within a polygonal projection and enriched stringcourse and stone voussoirs over windows, much like those at the United States Bank, this sadly mutilated building must have once been magnificent. Its plan is closely related to that of the Thomas Radcliffe House, also on George Street, built 1800–05. Margaret Manigault attended a party at the Radcliffe House in February, 1809: "Mrs. Radcliffe's ball . . . was really a splendid and well conducted affair. The house was well lighted . . . The stair case is very pretty, and the passage above remarkably large and well finished. It was . . . ornamented with festoons of flowers and flower pots from the green house shedding fragrant odours. . . . Hers was a Complete Ball—for it concluded with a magnificent supper at which near eighty persons were seated. The centre of it was adorned with an accumulation of iced plumb cakes in a kind of bower of natural flowers."[15] Radcliffe's house had superb cast plaster ornament which has been attributed to William Purviss, and some of it was salvaged and re-installed at the Dock Street Theatre after the house was demolished in 1938. The Radcliffe House also had graceful, arcaded three-tiered porches, which flanked its projecting entrance.

In the spring of 1808, at the surprisingly advanced age of seventy, Nathaniel Russell moved into a new house at 51 Meeting Street, a house similar in plan and decorative details to the Middleton-Pinckney House. Russell was born in Bristol, Rhode Island, in 1738, the son of a jurist who would later become that colony's Chief Justice. Russell came to Charleston about 1765 to follow the shipping business. A Tory sympathizer, Russell had been banished from South Carolina during the Revolution. Later repatriated, he became so important among the Northern-born merchants of Charleston that his contemporaries dubbed him "King of the Yankees." (Of the twenty-one leading commercial houses in Charleston between 1795 and 1816, only one was owned or managed by a native South Carolinian.)

Russell's house is a three-story brick structure with a low, hipped roof surmounted by a panelled balustrade. Arches over the recessed windows of the second story and stringcourse between floors are accented with bright red gauged brick. Lintels, sills, keystones and impost stripes are white marble, probably from New England. Long windows of the second, or principal, story lead out to a delicately wrought undulating iron balcony, which bears the initials of the owner in its design. The entrance is lit by an elaborately carved fanlight.

Above, left, and opposite, top: Frances Middleton/Thomas Pinckney House, 14 George Street, Charleston, 1797–1801. *Exterior photograph: South Carolina Historical Society.* Above, right, and opposite, bottom: Thomas Radcliffe House, George Street, Charleston, 1800–1805. *Interior photograph: Library of Congress, Exterior photograph: Charleston Museum*

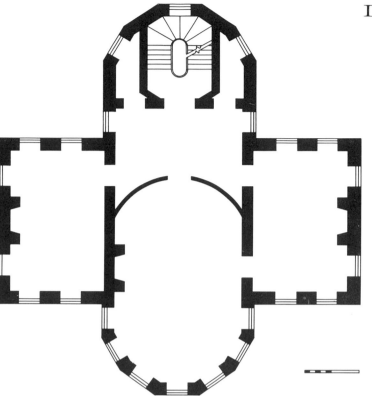

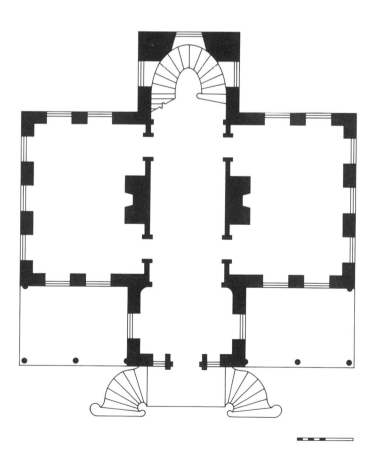

Nathaniel Russell House, 51 Meeting Street,
Charleston, 1808.

Nathaniel Russell House, side view from garden.

Nathaniel Russell House, view of stair from second
story landing.

Nathaniel Russell House, doorway into oval room
on second story.

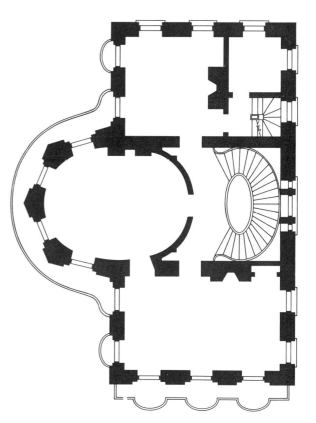

Plan of the Russell House.

This page and opposite: Nathaniel Russell House, views of oval room on second story.

Inside, a remarkable freestanding elliptical stair springs with apparent effortlessness from the first to the third story. The stair's handrail, composed of many neatly fitted mahogany pieces, makes a continuous, sinuous spiral to the attic. A separate service stair is located behind this principal one. The glory of the house is a favorite Adamesque device—oval rooms which project into the garden as a polygonal bay. All interior cornices, chair rails, door and window frames and mantels are enriched with cast plaster or carved wood. The designer of Russell's house remains unidentified. In 1819 William Faux called on the venerable Mr. Russell, who would die the following year, and found him "living in a splendid mansion, surrounded by a wilderness of flowers, and bowers of myrtles, oranges and lemons, smothered with fruits and flowers."[16]

A simpler house but one with a plan similar to Russell's house is Thomas Doughty's at 71 Anson Street, built about 1806. The entrance is hidden behind a brick wall with curvilinear parapet. A central room

Thomas Doughty House,
71 Anson Street, Charleston,
c. 1806.

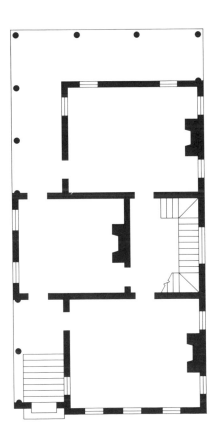

projects, like the oval room at Russell House, from the garden façade. Mantels bear plaster ornament, but elsewhere the decoration is carved wood.

Francis Simmons House, 14 Legare Street, Charleston, c. 1800.

The oldest of Charleston's famous many-galleried side piazzas, or porches, so distinctive and delightful, date from the immediate post-Revolutionary era. John Drayton described Charleston's characteristic dwellings of 1802: "The houses are, for the most part, of one or two stories. . . . Piazzas are generally attached to their southern front, as well for the convenience of walking therein during the day as for preventing the sun's too great influence on the interior part of the house."[17] Basil Hall, a retired naval officer, wrote in 1828: "What gives Charleston its peculiar character . . . is the veranda or piazza which embraces most of the houses on their southern side, and frequently also on those which face east and west. These are not clumsily put on but constructed in a light oriental style, extending from the ground to the very top, so that the rooms on each story enjoy the advantage of a shady, open walk."[18]

Despite much comment and commentary since the early 19th century, the evolution of these piazzas has yet to be considered carefully by architectural historians. It has often been suggested that they were brought to Carolina by the Barbadian planters who had been so influential in the early colony. The colonists had already learned how to ventilate and shade their dwellings in the sea islands, so the reasoning goes, and carried the idea with them to America. In fact, the early buildings of Carolina, the West Indies and other British "plantations" in the New World resembled the boxlike, hip-roofed, Dutch-inspired structures of Georgian England. The earliest surviving documented side porches of Charleston date from the post-Revolutionary period, long after the influence of the West Indian planters had ended. The dwellings of Charleston and the islands, which seem so similar today, date mainly from the 19th century. The addition of porches, designed to deflect the sun and provide space for open-air living, must have been a parallel development by English newcomers to Carolina and the West Indies after the early colonial period.

In November, 1700, to encourage the building of brick houses along the Bay, the provincial Assembly permitted landowners "to build Piazzas not exceeding Six Foot . . . with Steps in the said Piazzas up to the said House."[19] These were not side porches, but balconies running across the fronts of the buildings, as seen in the 1739 view of the city. The legislators were allowing homeowners to encroach on public property along the street fronts of their houses. After the fire of 1740, houses may have been deliberately narrowed and separated from each other to prevent future similar disasters. Thus the famous Charleston "single house" began to evolve and, with it, the side piazza. The principal entrance to the family quarters of these houses was moved to the side from the front of the building, and this entrance was now approached by a covered passageway, at first a one-story structure. The earliest references to piazzas suggest that they were useful rather than beautiful. In 1763 George Milligen-Johnston described Charleston: "There are about eleven Hundred Dwelling-Houses in the Town, built with Wood or Brick. Many of them have a genteel Appearance, though generally incumbered with Balconies or Piazzas."[20] In 1765 John Bartram, naturalist from Philadelphia, wrote: "The inhabitants of both Carolina and Georgia generally build piazzas on one or more sides of their houses which is very commodious in these hot climates. They screen off the violent scorching sunshine & draws the breeze finely and much conversation both sitting and walking is held in these."[21] It appears that soon after the Revolution, as their ornamental and functional possibilities became evident, the simple pre-Revolutionary one-story entrance porches were gradually enlarged and more elaborately designed. Significantly, the piazzas of Charleston are not merely appended to buildings: they serve as a processional, ceremonial entrance to the private quarters of the house.

In any case, graceful side piazzas, with slender Tuscan columns, shallow segmental arcading and boldly carved acanthus decorations, seem to have blossomed in Charleston about 1800. Philip Gadsden's house at 329 East Bay was built about 1800 for a factor, wharf owner and merchant. In addition to its graceful piazza, the house has a handsome Gibbs surround and ribbed keystone. Francis Simmons's house at 14 Legare Street was built about 1800 as the city residence of a John's Island planter. In addition to its fine porches, this house has an elaborate fence and gate which were added after 1816 by George Edwards, a later owner whose initials are incorporated in the design of the wrought iron. Thomas Heyward built a new house at 18 Meeting Street sometime between 1803 and 1806. His house has brick quoins at the angles, and the entablature of its superb piazza has not only a dentil and modillion cornice and acanthus leaf decorations but a Greek wave motif as well. James Mackie built 456 King Street in 1807, but it was enlarged by a later owner, William Aiken, Jr. in 1831. A portion of the graceful piazzas must date from the 1830's but probably repeats details of the original piazza of 1807. William Steele, a lumber merchant, built his house at 89 Beaufain Street in 1816–19. A remarkable carved marble frontispiece leads to an arcaded piazza. Each of these dwellings, all typical single houses with two rooms divided by a transverse stair hall, reflect the new Federal style. Walls are plastered above panelled dado, dainty plaster ornamentation appears on the mantels, around door architraves and along a frieze at the ceiling, stairs ascend in tight ellipses with balusters reduced to simple spindles.

Thomas Bennett, Jr., was the son of a gentleman architect, proprietor of lumber and rice mills and Governor of South Carolina between 1820 and 1822. He built a house at 69 Barre Street in 1822. The two-and-one-half story frame house, on its high brick basement, is a large version of a traditional single house. Located in what must have been at the time a suburban neighborhood, Bennett set his house behind a handsome picket fence. The piazza has segmental arches between the columns and acanthus leaves over the capitals and repeats the modillions of the eaves cornice with a bead-and-reel moulding. The attic gable, with its Venetian window, faces the street, and a pediment projects from the roof toward the garden. A visitor enters through a door with characteristic Federal elliptical fanlight and delicate sidelights into a hall with a free-standing elliptical staircase. The principal second-story front room has a marble mantel with a shelf supported by Ionic columns and a carved panel depicting a basket of grapes, all done in contrasting white and gray marble. Cornices throughout the house are variations of anthemia,

Above: Philip Gadsden House, 329 East Bay Street, Charleston, c. 1800. *Library of Congress.* Below: William Steele House, 89 Beaufain Street, Charleston, 1816–19.

Francis Simmons House, 14 Legare Street, Charleston, c. 1800.

William Steele House, 89 Beaufain Street, Charleston, 1816–19, interior doorway.

Thomas Bennett, Jr. House, 69 Barre Street, Charleston, 1802, side view from the garden. *Photograph by E. E. Soderholtz*

a classical ornament based on the honeysuckle and its leaves. Theodore Gaillard, a Cooper River rice planter and Charleston factor, built a two-and-one-half story frame house, with a central hall plan and high brick basement, at 60 Montague Street between 1800 and 1802. The house was much changed by a later owner, James Schoolbred, who, after purchasing it in 1819, added a new porch, marble steps and probably much of the lavish interior plaster decoration.

Patrick Duncan's house, now Ashley Hall School, was built at 172 Rutledge Avenue about 1816 by a Scotsman who came to Charleston as a shopkeeper and became a rich factor. The exterior is dominated by a monumental portico, elevated on an arcaded, rusticated basement, with three lancet-arched windows in its pediment. The fanlight entrance is set into an apse. This extraordinary design may have been the work of William Jay (1794–1837), a young English architect from Bath who appears to have reached Charleston, by way of Savannah, Georgia. In 1819 he designed "A Marine Villa" in the Gothic style on Sullivan's

Theodore Gaillard/James Schoolbred House, 60 Montague Street, Charleston, 1800–02, enlarged after 1819, first story ceiling medallion.

Theodore Gaillard/James Schoolbred House, view of second story chamber.

Theodore Gaillard/James Schoolbred House, interior view of first story chamber.

Patrick Duncan House, 172 Rutledge Avenue, Charleston, c. 1816.

Patrick Duncan House, view of stair from second story landing.

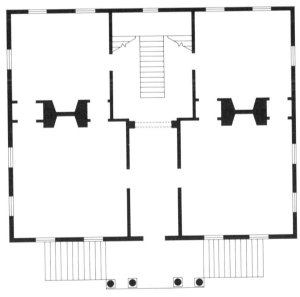

John Mark Verdier House, 801 East Bay Street, Beaufort, 1786. *Photograph: National Archives*

Island on the coast outside Charleston. In 1820 he exhibited "A Beautiful Model" of a series of buildings intended for the north and east sides of the public square at Broad and Meeting streets. After serving briefly on the Board of Public Works of South Carolina (Robert Mills redesigned several of Jay's courthouses before they had risen above their ground floors), Jay returned to England and later accepted a colonial office on the island of Mauritius in the Indian Ocean, where he died in 1837. The heavy mouldings and ornamental medallions inside Duncan's house were added by later owners, perhaps George A. Trenholm, later Secretary of the Confederate Treasury, who purchased the house in 1845.

Beaufort, on Port Royal Island, the first landing place of colonists bound for Carolina in 1670, was a center of cotton and rice production, prosperous enough to charter a college and four schools and pretentious enough to build a notable group of some five large similar houses. Three of these survive in more or less original appearance. All are two-story, hip-roofed structures on raised basements, with walls or foundations of tabby, a concretelike material made from oyster shells and lime. All have similar two-tiered, pedimented porticoes with slender Tuscan columns. Each has a central hall which widens at the rear to receive a single flight of stairs which rises to a landing, lit by a Venetian window, and then divides into two flights, returning to the second story against opposite sides of the hall. All have distinctive carved interior decoration as well as high-style cast plaster ornament. Indeed, if the dating of these buildings is correct, then Beaufort was ahead of Charleston in adopting the new Adam style.

Thomas Fuller's house at 1211 Bay Street, Beaufort, was built about 1780. It is a two-story structure, made of tabby, on a raised basement. John Mark Verdier's house at 881 Bay Street was built in 1786 for a Beaufort merchant and factor. It is a two-story frame structure on a raised tabby basement. Its original portico was altered after 1865, but early photographs have survived from the Civil War. Elizabeth Gough's house at 705 Washington Street was built about 1789. Like Fuller's house, it is a two-story structure made of tabby. And like Fuller's house and some others in Beaufort, it has a locally favored T-shaped plan, the rear chambers on either side of the central hall projecting beyond the width of the front façade.

When the Revolution against England had ended, another revolution in agriculture began in South Carolina. Without the imperial bounty supporting the price of indigo, the production of that staple was no longer profitable. Meanwhile, through new techniques of ditching and

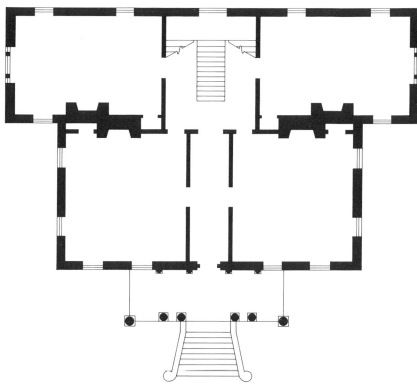

Above: Thomas Fuller House, 1211 Bay Street, Beaufort, c. 1780.
Below: Elizabeth Gough House, 705 Washington Street,
Beaufort, c. 1789.

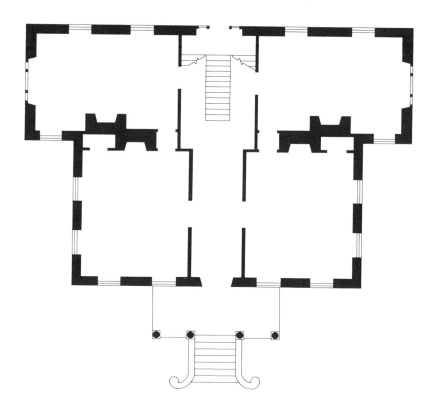

This page and opposite: John Mark Verdier House, general view and detail of carved wooden capital in stairhall.

John Mark Verdier House, second story chamber.

diking, the cultivation of rice was expanding from inland fresh water swamps to the vast delta closer to the ocean, and power-driven rice mills were speeding the processing of the crop. Then in 1793 the cotton gin was invented in nearby Georgia, making that crop an important staple which could be grown throughout the upper country. In 1792 construction of a canal between the Santee and Cooper rivers was begun and completed in 1800. Twenty miles long, thirty-five feet wide at the top and twenty feet wide at the bottom, with locks of brick and stone and paths for horses which pulled the boats, the canal provided passage for vessels up to fifty-four feet long and nine feet wide. At last, the interior of South Carolina was linked to Charleston.

In the interior of South Carolina, Adam decoration, which had been sleek and sophisticated in Charleston, became exuberant and fanciful. Instead of applying cast plaster ornament to mantels and door and window frames, local craftsmen created highly personal designs in wood. In 1939 the building of two reservoirs, which would soon flood twenty square miles, called attention to an important group of distinctive early dwellings in the Upper St. John's Parish of Berkeley County, an area of rich cotton and rice lands developed after the Revolution.[22] Many of these houses, built by newly rich cotton planters, had unusual plans of a local type and outstanding carved wood decoration, much of it probably executed by one talented craftsman. Most of these houses were two-story, hip-roofed frame structures on elevated brick basements. In place of a conventional central hall, two separate front doors led into two large chambers. Behind these chambers, there was a rear stair hall, flanked by two smaller rooms. The interiors were decorated with wonderful carved wood, sometimes covering the entire chimney breasts.

Peter Gaillard was a former rice and indigo planter who began raising cotton in the Upper St. John's area in the mid-1790's. Construction of his house, The Rocks, near the village of Eutaw Springs, is recorded in his daybook between 1803 and 1805.[23] On May 11, 1803, his workers began to saw cypress and make shingles. In September, they began to make bricks. One carpenter was hired in October, another in November and a third in December. On February 22, 1804, the foundations were begun. In April, after the cotton planting had been completed, the house frame was raised. During the summer, two chimneypieces "to be done in a genteel but plain style" were ordered from Rhode Island. The house was finished in April, 1805. The two principal rooms have reeded chair rails, bold modillion cornices and the two chimneypieces from New England, with pairs of reeded pilasters supporting a full entablature and broken pediment. In 1942 The Rocks was moved about two miles, so that it would not be destroyed by the rising waters of the reservoir.

Frederick Augustus Porcher, in his memoir of life in this neighborhood of Upper St. John's, Berkeley, wrote that The Rocks was "the Standard Plantation," a model for friends and relations when they built houses and managed their farms.[24] Thomas Porcher, the brother-in-law of Peter Gaillard, built Ophir about 1810, located in the vicinity of Pinopolis, some twenty-five miles from The Rocks. Ophir shared the unusual plan of The Rocks, with its twin front doors and no central front hall, as well as carefully carved wood decoration. Thomas Porcher, Jr., son of the builder of Ophir, built another lavishly decorated house, White Hall, near Pinopolis, in 1822.

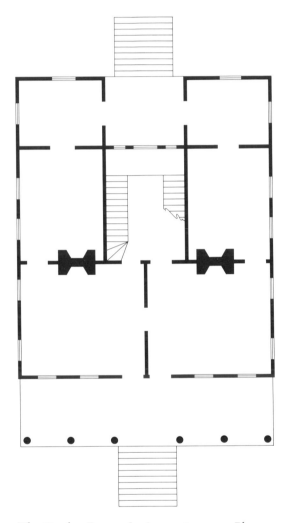

The Rocks, Eutaw Springs, 1803–05. Photograph shows the house before it was moved in 1942. *South Carolina Art Association*

Joseph Palmer built Springfield, located near Eutaw Springs, scarcely two miles from The Rocks, in 1817. Palmer recorded the progress of construction in his account book: "Mr. Champlin commenced on Monday October the 20th, 1817, to build a dwelling house for me 46 feet by 40 feet with a wing at each end 22 x 16 feet at $60 per Month. The framing of the house was begun Oct. 21 and finished the 20th of November."[25] The house was altogether completed in June, 1818, a two-story frame structure on an elevated brick basement with gable roof, central hall plan and gabled wings whose doors have semicircular fanlights and flanking windows, all set under a continuous entablature and full pediment. Frederick Augustus Porcher wrote in his memoirs: "Springfield . . . a noble mansion . . . was built upon brick pillars about

he Rocks, chimneypieces in first story chambers.

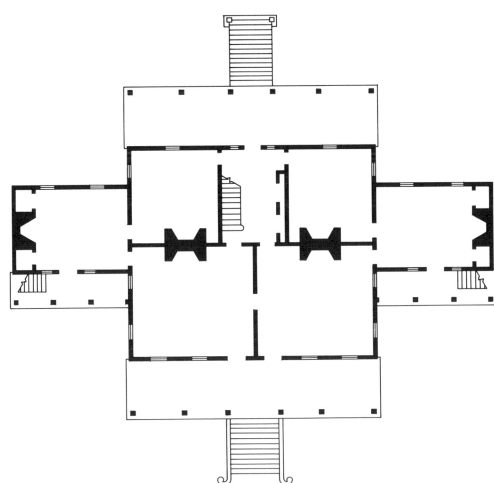

Springfield, Eutaw Springs, 1817.
Carolina Art Association

ringfield, chimneypiece. *Library of Congress*

Blueford, Pineville, c. 1817, chimneypiece.
South Carolina Historical Society

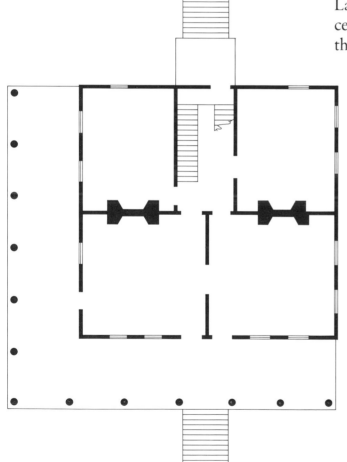

ten feet in height. . . . The main building was about fifty feet in length by forty in width . . . on which side ran a wide piazza, and at both the east and the west end of the main building was a wing, each about twenty-five by twenty feet, which furnished commodious chambers, one for the master and mistress of the house and the other for whomsoever they might for the time appropriate it. From the piazza you entered two large and elegantly furnished rooms, in both of which was a gorgeous display of carved woodwork. The windows were bracketed, and the whole chimney piece enclosed with wooden panels, all of which were so elaborately worked that the chisel seemed to have cut into every square line of the wood. This was the design and the performance of a Yankee carpenter who astonished the people by his skill."[26] Springfield was destroyed in 1940.

The "Yankee carpenter" at Springfield, George Champlin, was probably responsible for the excellent carving at Blueford, built about the same time near Pineville, and Lawson's Pond, built about 1823 outside Eutaw Springs for Charles Cordes Porcher. Like The Rocks and Ophir, Lawson's Pond has twin front doors, two large front chambers and no central front hall. It seems probable, from their incomplete appearance, that entablatures were intended for the exterior windows but were

Lawson's Pond, Eutaw Springs, c. 1823.

Lawson's Pond, first story chamber.

Lawson's Pond, detail of door in first story chamber.

never installed. The unpainted black cypress exterior does not prepare a visitor for the beauty of the interior. Doors and windows carry complete entablatures, with dentil cornice, a frieze decorated with sunbursts and an architrave with reeded panels. Wainscotting, doors, mantels and stair have been painted to resemble marble.

In isolated communities, everyone with money and a taste for fine building knew and copied the homes of their relations and neighbors. Another group of distinctive early 19th century houses, all with beautiful arcaded porches and central hall plans, was built in the west-central portion of South Carolina, in territory stretching from Abbeville to Edgefield, settled principally by settlers from Virginia and North Carolina. George Lester's house in Saluda County, just south of the Saluda River, was probably built about 1800, though the date March 10, 1826,

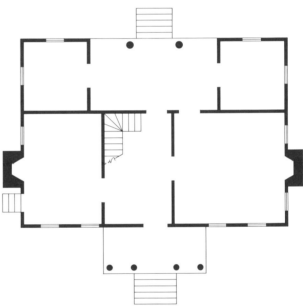

George Lester House, Saluda County, c. 1800.

has been scratched in the chimney. Its arcaded porch, though somewhat decayed, is elegant, with slender, tapering Tuscan columns, a carefully detailed cornice, bull's-eye window in the pediment and dainty rail and balusters. The interior is sheathed with horizontal flush boards over gougework chair rail and panelled dado. John Blocker's house, Cedar Grove, was built about 1800 just north of Edgefield, a neat little village of some thirty families at the time. The elegance of its two-tiered ar-

Cedar Grove, Edgefield, c. 1800–05.

caded portico has been diminished by the removal of some details, but the entrance leads into a remarkable barrel-vaulted hall, whose ceiling is constructed of flush boards nailed to a framework suspended from the floor joists above. The walls are finished with flush boards above a chair rail and panelled dado, except in the right front parlor, which retains an early hand-painted French wallpaper.

James Lomax, Jr. built his house in Greenwood County near the village of Hodges between 1809 and 1812, facing what was at the time the main road between Clemson and Augusta. Its arcaded front porch has an unusual arrangement of four bays over six bays. Stony Point, north of Greenwood, was begun in 1818 by William Smith, who had come from Culpepper County, Virginia, in 1793. Its Flemish bond brickwork, jerkinhead roof and jack arches over the windows recall 18th century Virginia. Still unfinished when Smith died in 1824, the house was completed by his son Joel in 1829. The two-tiered arcaded portico, with an elliptical window in its pediment, suffers from some modern alterations. Sylvania, one of South Carolina's most delightful small houses, was built by John Hearst in 1825 near Bradley, on the west side of the old Abbeville-Edgefield stage road. Hearst's father had come from Ireland to Charleston in 1766. A large pedimented dormer, with a Venetian window, projects from the gable roof. The interiors have marvellous painted decoration. Hall walls are painted with a wide,

Left: Stony Point, Greenwood vicinity, 1818–29.
Right: James Lomax, Jr. House, Hodges, 1809–12.

Sylvania, Bradley, 1825. This page and opposite: exterior view and stairhall.

Sylvania, graining and marbling in first story chamber.

fanciful garland of grape vines, and doors and dadoes have been grained and marbleized. The last and perhaps greatest of these houses was Edgewood, built at Edgefield in 1829 by Francis Pickens, congressman, Governor of South Carolina and notable advocate of states' rights. As originally built, a central main house and flanking dependencies, all with arcaded porches, were connected by raised, covered passageways. Fortunately, this building was measured about 1900, before the house was moved to nearby Aiken and much changed.

Edgewood, Edgefield, 1829.

In the 1820's, the Roman inspiration behind the Federal style was often expressed in greater monumentality. One of South Carolina's most remarkable buildings is the Borough House at Stateburg, at the time a village of eight houses, two stores and three or four shops on the hills near the Wateree River. In 1792 Thomas Hooper, a North Carolinian, purchased a building of undocumented 18th century origin. The inscription on an early land plat identifies the property as "Mrs. Hooper's house, formerly the tavern." An ink sketch on a later map of 1809 illustrates the original building: a two-story frame structure with end chimneys and shed rooms at the ends of a long front porch. In 1820 William Wallace Anderson, a graduate of the University of Pennsylvania Medical School who had come from Maryland to South Carolina in 1810, inherited the old tavern, and in 1821 the transformation of the old building was begun. The wooden shed rooms were removed and replaced with gabled wings. The original end chimneys were taken down to make room for doors to the new wings. Two-tiered porticoes, with Roman Ionic columns, were added to the principal façades. The entire structure, old and new, was finished with a stucco-like coating. Today the enlarged tavern, with its splendid portico, seems to resemble one of the elegant villas in Palladio's famous *Four Books of Architecture*.

"Mrs. Hooper's House, formerly the tavern," sketched on an 1809 map. *Private Collection*

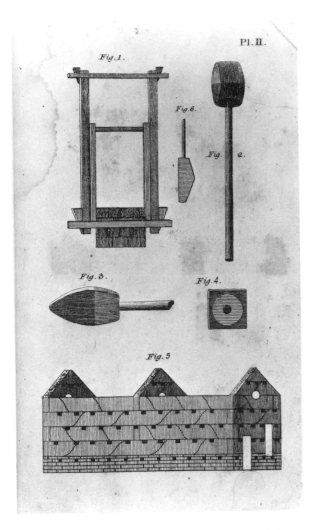

Pisé de terre construction, illustrated in S. W. Johnson's *Rural Economy* (New Brunswick, 1806). *Private Collection*

The wings are unusual for the method of their construction. Dr. Anderson brought with him to South Carolina a copy of S. W. Johnson's *Rural Economy*, an extraordinary work published at New Brunswick, New Jersey, in 1806. In this eccentric treatise, the author explored viticulture, turnpikes and *pisé de terre* construction, a technique of building walls with beaten earth. "The walls, except for the foundation," he wrote, "are entirely of the commonest soil, taken from a bank by the road side."[27] A foundation of stone or brick, some two feet high, is erected. Then walls of clay are built by pounding a few inches of soil at a time into a wooden mould. As layer after layer is beaten, the wood mould is raised and door and window frames inserted as necessary. The interior is finished with lath and plaster, the exterior with a mixture of limestone, sand and water. These buildings were to be practical, economical and healthful. "Such buildings may with strictest veracity be said to be fire-proof, cheap, durable, warm in winter, cool in summer, healthful, being impervious to moisture . . . [and] capable of receiving any ornaments of stone or brick, and of being painted as fancy directs." Inspired by Johnson's *Rural Economy*, Dr. Anderson was also responsible for the *pisé de terre* construction of the nearby Church of the Holy Cross, designed by Edward C. Jones of Charleston in 1850.

In 1827 John C. Calhoun enlarged a frame two-story house which had been built about 1803 by Dr. James McElhenny on an 1100-acre plantation near Clemson. Calhoun, born in South Carolina in 1782, graduated from Yale in 1804 and then spent forty years as a congressman, secretary of war, vice president, secretary of state and senator. In 1825 Calhoun had bought the farm and named it Fort Hill, honoring an old fort built on the property during the Revolution. Like the portico added to the South Carolina Society Hall, Charleston, by Frederick Wesner in 1825 and like the Farmers' Society Hall, built on the village green at Pendleton between 1826 and 1828, Calhoun's Fort Hill used Roman details for monumental effect. In a world of few trained designers, local housewrights inevitably copied what was familiar, and so throughout the Greek Revival period which was soon to follow many Carolina builders continued to combine Roman as well as Greek details.

Borough House, Stateburg, 18th century house remodeled in 1821.

South Carolina Society Hall, 72 Meeting Street, Charleston, 1802, portico added 1825.

Robert Mills was born at Charleston in 1781, the son of a tailor. He later described himself as "the first native American who directed his studies to architecture as a profession."[1] (The first architecture school in America was not opened until 1866.) Mills probably received his first impressions of architecture as a profession from James Hoban, when that Irish designer was working in Charleston between 1790 and 1792. In 1800, at the age of nineteen, Mills moved to Washington to work for Hoban, then in charge of the U.S. Capitol. From him, Mills would have learned how to construct provincial Palladian buildings, much like the large public buildings of colonial Charles Town and the design with which Hoban won the competition for the President's House at Washington in 1793. An old-fashioned design surely adapted from James Gibbs's *Book of Architecture*, the White House could be easily mistaken for a fairly typical mid-18th century English country house.

At the end of 1801, the state legislature of South Carolina established the South Carolina College at Columbia. The following March, trustees for the new institution advertised for designs, offering $300 for "the best original plan of a College."[2] It was to be made of stone or brick, with lodging and class rooms for one hundred students and three professors and to cost no more than $50,000. The trustees received some ten proposals from designers in Maryland, Connecticut, North Carolina, Rhode Island and New Jersey—and from the youthful Robert Mills, who signed himself "Architect and Practical Builder & Eng., Washington, 1802." Mills's submission was a cautious, conventional late Georgian plan, typical of college buildings in colonial America, and indicates that he had yet to develop an architectural personality. The building committee accepted no one plan and the prize money was divided between Mills and a "Mr. Clark." Elements of Mills's design were incorporated into the final scheme, and it appears that Mills was then hired to make final drawings for the college buildings, based on the committee's version of the designs which had been submitted.

In January, 1805, the South Carolina College opened with two professors and nine students. Rutledge College, the first building, had been completed, and DeSaussure College, a similar structure facing it, was still an unfinished shell of masonry walls and roof. In November, 1805, Edward Hooker of Connecticut visited Columbia and described the new building: "The central parts are designed for the Chapel, Library, Philosophical Chamber, Recitation Rooms, &c.—the wings are designed for scholars' mansion rooms. The chapel occupies the two lower stories of the central building on the right, and is in a beautiful style of workmanship both within and without. The Library room above is

V.
Robert Mills in South Carolina, 1802–1837

158

supported by four stately Tuscan columns, which rise from the area of the chapel with considerable majesty, and give to the rooms an appearance of grandeur. The wings are three stories high, and are divided into twelve mansion rooms each, and twenty-four bedrooms."[3]

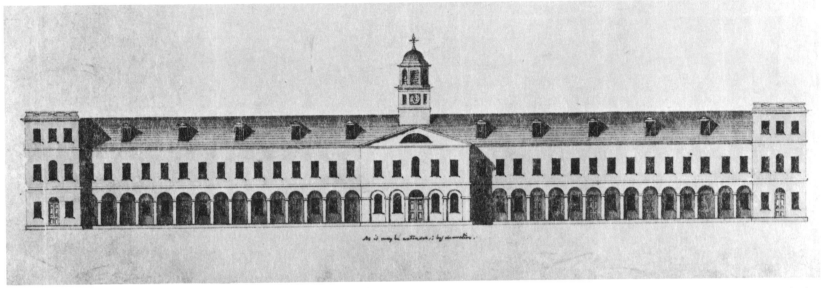

South Carolina College, Columbia, design by Robert Mills, 1802. *South Carolina Department of Archives and History*

In Washington, Mills met Thomas Jefferson, who encouraged the young Carolinian. He hired Mills to make drawings of designs for his home, Monticello, outside Charlottesville, Virginia. Jefferson, a lover of books and buildings, owned what was probably the finest architecture library in the country at the time. Mills wrote: "As there were no architecture books to be had, Mr. Jefferson kindly offered me the use of his library."[4] So much more than a country squire and gentleman amateur, Jefferson also introduced Mills to new architectural ideas. In July, 1802, Jefferson wrote a letter of introduction for Mills to Charles Bulfinch of Boston. Jefferson was a serious architectural theorist. He had little regard for colonial buildings, like those of Hoban, which he viewed as clumsy imitations of classical architecture. He rejected Adamesque design as the style of conservative, class-conscious, effete, English-loving Federalists. Instead, Jefferson wanted strong, simple architecture for America. He looked to Palladio as his model—not the debased Palladianism of England but the Renaissance original. When Jefferson was sent to France between 1784 and 1789, he saw firsthand the Roman antiquities he already loved, but, more important, he was propelled into the vanguard of "modern" architecture when he saw the revolutionary neoclassical architecture of the late 18th century in France. Attempting to create a new public architecture in an era of rapid social change, these designers had stripped Roman architecture of unnecessary ornament and reduced it to pure geometric forms—the cube, the sphere and the pyramid. The work of these visionary Frenchmen appealed instinctively to Jefferson, the rationalist and idealist, just as Palladio had appealed to him as a bibliophile. When Jefferson returned to Virginia, he tore down parts of Monticello, originally a Palladian building, and rebuilt it more in line with current French fashion.

Jefferson and Mills continued to exchange letters until Jefferson's death in 1826, and the elder's architectural tastes were a compelling, lasting influence on the young man. Roman in detail and form but so much simpler than the originals, Jefferson's buildings were generally brick structures with white porticoes of four unfluted Roman Doric or Tuscan columns, lunette windows, plain entablatures and raised basements. From Jefferson, Mills developed his predilection for simplified Roman forms and an understanding that the design of buildings, public or private, must not only please the eye but serve practical needs as well. Jeffersonian classicism was a style well suited for the public buildings of the young Republic, so many of which Robert Mills would later design—and in a style very reminiscent of Jefferson.

When Mills entered the architectural office of Benjamin H. Latrobe about 1803, where he remained off and on till about 1815, he came under the spell of a third, still more progressive, architectural force. Latrobe had come to Virginia in 1796 and established himself at Philadelphia by the end of 1798. Latrobe submitted a plan for the South Carolina College. Personally selected by Jefferson, Latrobe received an appointment as Surveyor of Public Buildings in Washington in 1802. Latrobe was a fully-trained professional. Unlike Hoban, who came from provincial Ireland, Latrobe came from the England of Sir John Soane. In England, the highly ornamented style of Robert Adam was already becoming old-fashioned, though not yet so in America. Soane was attempting to create spatial effects freed of unnecessary ornament, like the fiercely rational French architects observed by Jefferson. The bold geometry of these buildings, facilitated by sophisticated engineering, was expressed by springing vaults, thin, flat surfaces and finely chiseled decoration. Following the avant garde of English taste, Soane turned more and more to Greek models for elements of his designs.

From Latrobe, who called himself a "bigoted Greek," Mills learned about Greek architecture long before it became fashionable in America. Like Latrobe, who used Greek as well as Roman forms in his designs, Mills used them both—and often confused them in his writings, too. Like Latrobe, Mills was an engineer as well as designer, making a speciality of civic projects and internal improvements. Like Latrobe, who spent fifteen years working on Federal buildings in Washington, Mills was appointed Federal Architect by President Jackson in 1836. Like Latrobe, Soane and Jefferson as well, Mills's architecture emphasized simple, strong geometric forms shed of unnecessary ornament. Mills's work expressed the classicism of Jefferson, with its devotion to Roman forms, enhanced by Latrobe's knowledge of Greek architecture and sophisticated engineering, all simplified by American conditions. With surprising frequency, many of Mills's buildings bear striking, specific resemblances to those of his teacher Latrobe, who once wrote of him: "Mills . . . came to me too late to acquire principles of taste. He is a copyist and is fit for nothing else."[5]

Circular Church, Charleston, 1804–06, steeple 1838. Left: Drawing by Jones and Lee, c. 1852. *South Carolina Historical Society.* Right: The ruins, photographed c. 1865. *Library of Congress*

Robert Mills's first completed work was the Circular Church in Charleston, begun in 1804 and finished in 1806. (The building was modified in 1838 and 1853 and destroyed by fire in 1861.) The church was a vast domed hall, ninety feet in diameter, entered through a portico of six monumental columns. Inside, an almost continuous gallery surrounded the large auditorium, paved with flagstone and lit by a low lantern at the center of a flat dome. Outside, round-headed windows were set into recessed arches. Mills described the church himself: "A rotunda of near 90 feet diameter surmounted by a dome, crowned by a lanthorn light. From that part of the rotunda which faces the west, a square projection runs out, supporting a tower. Before this rises a portico of six columns, surmounted by a pediment which forms the façade of the building. A double arcade is carried all round to the circumscribing walls, the openings of which constitute the windows. . . . A light gallery sweeps nearly a complete circle around the room and presents the appearance of a great settee, the columns supporting it being of a character suited to convey an idea of this kind. In the original design of this building a steeple was contemplated, which has not yet been erected; the tower part is, however, built."[6] Like Latrobe's famous Baltimore Cathedral, 1804, the Circular Church was dominated by a vast segmental dome with a colossal portico and round-headed windows set into recessed arches.

Significantly, the building committee had already decided, in December, 1803, to erect a church with a circular plan even before Mills had been hired as its architect. Several designers, notably Jefferson, had designed great domes as an emblem of the young Republic for public buildings. As a practical matter, a big round room served the needs of eloquent, emotion-stirring preachers in a democratic age. Unlike the old traditional church of the English Wren-Gibbs type, which presented the minister as a remote religious celebrant at the distant end of a chancel, this new church placed the preacher nearer his flock, where he could be more easily seen and heard. After Abiel Abbot, a minister from Andover, Massachusetts, preached at the Circular Church in November, 1818, he called it "the most extraordinary building . . . in the United States." The aisles, he wrote, were "broad enough to accommodate negro worshippers & carpeted to prevent echo. . . . The vast gulf of space before the speaker is filled by pews & galleries."[7] Mills later designed other domed churches: the Samson Street Church in Philadelphia, 1808–09, the Monumental Church in Richmond, 1812, the Octagonal Church in Philadelphia, 1813, and the First Baptist Church in Baltimore, 1818.

Though it opened in May, 1806, the Circular Church was considered incomplete and imperfect, even by the architect himself who wrote: "The modern Doric style pervades this building, which is to be regretted, particularly in reference to its great portico. Had the Greek proportions been adopted (as recommended by the architect) the effect of the whole building would have been much more interesting."[8] It seems likely that a powerful and opinionated building committee, headed by David Ramsay, a famous early historian of South Carolina, had vetoed some of the proposals of their young architect, then only twenty-three years old, and substituted slight "modern Doric," that is Roman Doric, columns, in place of more robust Greek ones. Designing the balcony like "a great settee," Mills had tapered its supporting columns from top to bottom like the legs of a giant Sheraton sofa, a conceit which left the congregation more puzzled than pleased. A more serious complaint was that the dome seemed too flat, too low, too heavy and always ready to collapse. Richard Yeadon, a Charleston newspaper editor and lawyer, complained in 1853: "The first question which suggested itself to the minds of the beholders was not 'Why it does not rise?' but, to the contrary, 'Why it does not fall?'. . . In this church, speculation is always busy as to the chances of its falling about one's ears!"[9] The services were hampered by echoes in the auditorium, said to be Charleston's coldest hall in winter and hottest in summer. The lack of a steeple also provoked ridicule, like this couplet of the day: "Charleston is a pious place and full of pious people / They built a church on Meeting Street but could not raise the steeple!"[10]

In 1838 Charles F. Reichardt was hired to add the missing spire, and in 1853 architects Edward C. Jones and Francis D. Lee made other alterations. These improvements endured only eight years, for the church was destroyed by fire at the end of 1861. On December 16, word of fire in downtown Charleston reached Emma Holmes in the suburbs: "The terror! the misery & desolation which has swept like a hurricane over our once fair city. . . . Sparks . . . floated in the air . . . like falling stars. It was terrifically beautiful!" The next day, she walked among the ruins of the Circular Church. "The walls . . . are perfect and part of the steeple [is] still standing, and, with the moonlight streaming through the windows, . . . the effect was beautiful and reminded us of the Coliseum."[11] Despite its acknowledged original imperfections, subsequent alterations and ultimate destruction, the Circular Church remains one of the most famous buildings of Charleston and one of Mills's most genuinely creative works.

In March, 1804, while the Circular Church was still under construction, Mills prepared plans and specifications for enlargements and modifications to venerable St. Michael's Church.[12] The plans for extending the east end of the structure, with new altar, pulpit and reading desk, were presented to the vestry on March 11. In July, estimates for the

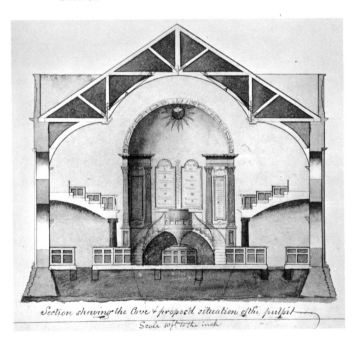

St. Michael's Church, Charleston, proposed additions drawn by Robert Mills, 1804. *St. Michael's Church*

work were requested, but the plans were never executed. The surviving drawings indicate Mills's skill as an architectural draftsman and give us some idea of interior details which might have been used at the Circular Church.

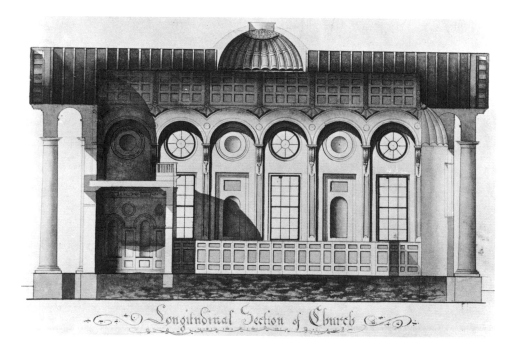

Episcopal Church, John's Island, elevation and section for proposed church drawn by Robert Mills, c. 1804. *Charleston Library Society*

At about the same time, Mills submitted proposals for the Episcopal Church on John's Island near Charleston.[13] The church was to be forty-two feet long and twenty-six and a half feet wide, plus the porticoes, the exterior walls two bricks thick, laid in Flemish bond and stuccoed. The columns and entablature were to be brick, the steps and door and window sills stone, the floors of aisles and vestibule to be laid with black marble squares. A copper-clad dome on a blue slate roof would have a skylight. Below a cove ceiling, there would be twenty-two pews, with raised panels on one side, "with front Edges rounded off and Ogee Supports." A small Gallery, "purpos'd entirely for Servants," extended over the vestibule. This church was never constructed, but Mills's drawings and specifications have survived.

Meanwhile, Mills remained in Philadelphia, working for Latrobe, until 1815, when he moved to Baltimore. But his involvement with the architecture of his native South Carolina continued. In 1818 he designed the First Baptist Church at 61 Church Street in Charleston. The drawing is signed "Baltimore Jany 2 1818." The building was constructed between 1819 and 1822. Mills described it in 1826: "The best specimen of correct taste in architecture of the modern buildings of this

First Baptist Church, drawing by Robert Mills, 1818. *First Baptist Church*

city. It is purely Greek in its style, simply grand in its proportions, and beautiful in its detail. The plan is of the temple form, divided into four parts. . . . The façade presents a portico of four massy columns of the lightest proportions of the Doric, surmounted by a pediment. Behind this portico . . . rises an attic story squared up to the height of the roof and crowned by a cupola or belfry. . . . Around three sides of the nave a double colonnade extends, rises up to the roof, and supports the galleries. The lower order of the columns is Doric, the upper Ionic; each with their regular entablatures; the whole finished in a rich chaste style and producing, from the unity of the design, a very pleasant effect."[14] Though he described the church as "purely Greek in its style," Mills was confusing Greek and Roman details, as he often did, for the portico has Roman Doric columns, the façade has semicircular arches and the interior has Roman Ionic capitals.

For Camden, a thriving trading town on the Wateree River with 300 houses and 2000 inhabitants, Mills designed the Bethesda Presbyterian Church. It was begun in 1820 and dedicated in October, 1822. The principal façade of this small Roman temple, its portico supported by Tuscan columns and a full entablature, is laid in Flemish bond. Two round-headed doorways at the side of the portico lead into the building. These doors and round-headed windows are decorated with brightly colored rubbed brick and the walls above them are embellished with rectangular plaster panels, a favorite Adamesque device. The pulpit is located behind the center of the front wall, and flanking aisles lead to pews which face forward. Pews and floor rise as they recede from the pulpit. The resulting change in floor level, some three feet between front and rear, seems to have forced the architect to make awkward adjustments in the details of the exterior side walls. The windows were raised to accommodate the higher floor, placing the tops of the windows and the related decorative panels out of line with those of the front and forcing the elimination of the entablature used at the front façade. However, the church has a cheerful delicacy which is not characteristic of Mills's usually serious and severe designs.

Another building in the Camden vicinity associated historically and stylistically with Mills is Mulberry Grove, built as the winter residence of James Chestnut, an extensive planter and state legislator. Chestnut, whose wife had come from Philadelphia, hired a Philadelphia master carpenter, David Bartling, to build his house. Between 1820 and 1822 Bartling was supervising the work both at Bethesda Church and Mulberry Grove. He reached Camden in May, 1820, submitting bills to Chestnut in May, 1821, for "261 days @ $3 = $783" and May, 1822

First Baptist Church, 61 Church Street, Charleston, 1818–22, exterior view.

First Baptist Church, interior view.

Bethesda Presbyterian Church, Camden, 1820–22.

for "234 days @ \$3 = \$702," and died there in August, 1822. William Strickland, who had worked with Mills in the Philadelphia office of Benjamin H. Latrobe and who would design the main building of the College of Charleston in 1828, may have been the architect of Mulberry, for Bartling wrote to Chestnut on March 20, 1820, that he was preparing "to commence your business" and that "Mr. Strickland will have the other drawings ready, which I shall likewize bring with me."[15]

In plan, Mulberry Grove is a perfect square, with front and side walls of the same length, laid in Flemish bond, with a gable roof, originally slate. In the central hall, door architraves are flanked by fluted, engaged Roman Ionic columns. The arch which leads to the rear of the hall is supported by freestanding columns of similar design, which are elliptical, not circular, in plan. The step ends of the circular stair are decorated with scrolls and stylized flowers. The doors of the principal story are hung with silver-plated hinges. The chimneys of the main rooms have marble mantels, which were probably shipped from Philadelphia, like the cast-iron firebacks which are marked "Cumberland Furnace." A separate kitchen and laundry stood behind the main house.

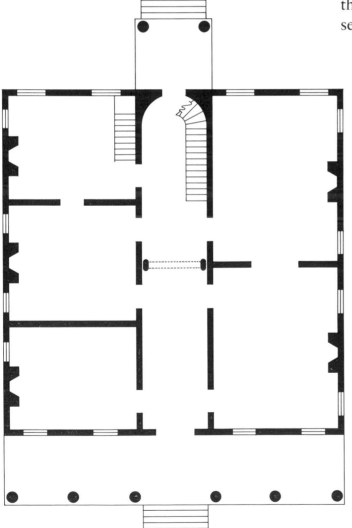

Mulberry Grove, Camden vicinity, 1820–22, a 19th century photograph. *South Caroliniana Library, University of South Carolina*

Mulberry Grove, exterior view.

Mulberry Grove, detail of hall.

In December, 1820, Mills returned to Charleston from Baltimore. South Carolina was embarked on an ambitious program of public works, spending more than $1.5 million on canals, dams, locks and the State Road, a railway from Charleston to Columbia, between 1818 and 1828. Mills received an appointment from the South Carolina legislature as one of two paid members of the five-member Board of Public Works with the title of Acting Commissioner. In December, 1822, when the legislature abolished the Board, Mills was made Superintendent of Public Buildings, an office he held for one year. From 1824 to 1828 he continued to assist with the design of public buildings, while working in private practice. Recent research indicates that Mills designed at least fourteen courthouses, fourteen jails and nine circular brick powder magazines outside Charleston during this period.[16] Mills's influence on others has led to misattributions.

Courthouse, Camden, drawing by Robert Mills, 1825. *South Carolina Historical Society*

In fact, only one drawing of a courthouse by Robert Mills and one set of his specifications are known to have survived. Courthouses designed by Mills were built at Greenville (1821, demolished 1924), Newberry (1821, demolished 1851), Georgetown (1822, enlarged c. 1854), Marion (1822, demolished 1851), Bennettsville (1822, demolished c. 1850), Kingstree (1822, enlarged 1853–54), York (1822, enlarged 1851), Conwayborough (1823), Union (1823, demolished c. 1912), Darlington (1824, enlarged 1853), Chesterfield (1824, burned 1865), Camden (1825, altered c. 1845), Orangeburg (1826–28, burned 1865), Abbeville (1828, demolished c. 1852). Most of these courthouses were built as gable-ended temple-like structures, with pedimented porticoes, supported by Tuscan columns, resting on arcaded basements. A low, stone-vaulted ground story contained offices and fireproof storage, and a tall principal story contained a courtroom. Mills's specifications for the courthouse at Chesterfield indicate the careful construction of these buildings. On the ground story, four groin-vaulted offices were divided by a central barrel-vaulted hall. The low vaults were to be reinforced with concealed iron rods. The stuccoed brick columns of the portico were to be painted marble color, with stone bases and capitals. Windows of the principal story were to have "neat stone arching" and the entrance was to have "fancy transom lights." Exterior brick walls were to be stuccoed and then painted brick color and neatly penciled with white lead. "The materials are to be of the best that the country can afford," Mills wrote.[17]

South Carolina was still a sparsely settled state, its forests punctuated by district villages, generally located on important rivers, each consisting of a courthouse, jail, perhaps fifty houses, a few stores and church. Mills's jewel-like temples of democracy dominated these hodgepodge hamlets and must have been admired by all as carefully planned models of classical architecture. Mills described the courthouse at Camden in 1826: "An elegant court-house . . . superior in its design to any in the state, both for convenience of accommodation, beauty and permanency. Its facade presents a grand portico of six Ionic columns, spreading the whole extent of the building, and rising so high that the main roof will cover it and constitute its pediment. The offices (six in number) occupy the lower or basement story, arched with brick and made fire-proof. . . . Four columns rise in this court-room, carrying their imposts, between which springs a grand arched ceiling, the whole width of the room, and extending its entire length."[18] Mills described his courthouse at York: "An elegant structure, built of stone and brick. The offices in the basement story are made fire-proof. The court and jury rooms on the principal floor are communicated with by a double flight of granite steps, ascending to a portico of the Doric order. . . . The court-room . . . is spacious, convenient, and airy, amphitheatrical in its form, with a segment spherical ceiling. The jury rooms are so arranged that the space above them and the vestibule serves the purposes of a roomy gallery for spectators."[19]

Mills designed a Public Record Office at Charleston for the State in 1822.[20] Bids were advertised in April and the cornerstone was laid in May. It was completed at last in 1826. Its exterior is dominated by two monumental Greek Doric porticoes, each with a pediment and four columns resting on an arcaded basement. The exterior is finished with stucco, scored and painted to resemble blocks of stone. Mills described the building: "It is designed in the simple Greek Doric style, without any ornament, except that afforded by the porticoes which face each front. These porticoes are each composed of four massy columns three and a half feet diameter, raised on an arcade. The columns rise the whole height of the building (comprising two stories) surmounted by their entablature, and crowned with a pediment, which, extending entirely across the building, meet together in the middle. The remaining part of the building, on each side, constitutes wings to the centre, falling below the apex of the pediment."[21]

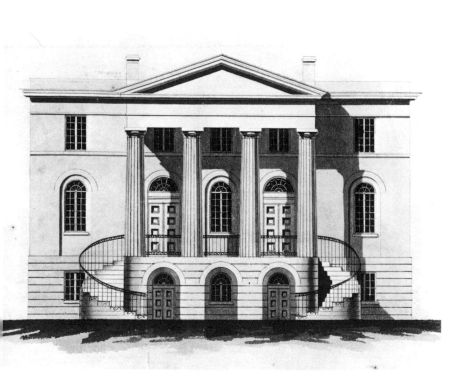

Public Record Office, Meeting Street, Charleston, 1822–26, drawing by Robert Mills and plan.
Drawing: South Carolina Historical Society

Public Record Office, exterior view.

Though often described as the first fireproof building in America, the Record Office was designed only to be fire-resistant. The location of the structure was carefully planned, so that it would be located at the corner of a public square, unlikely to catch fire from nearby buildings. The walls and ceilings of the first two stories are barrel- or groin-vaulted brick construction. The windows, their frames, shutters and casements, are iron. The stairs are built of stone, with handrails and balusters of iron, and the halls are paved with stone. Yet there are fireplaces in all but four of the building's twenty-four rooms, and wood is used for the lathing, joists and rafters of the third story ceiling and the copper-sheathed roof.

Alas, John George Spidle, the supervising builder, modified the original design shown in Mills's elegant drawing of its principal front. The portico's columns were not fluted, the second story windows were elongated and a stringcourse between first and second stories was eliminated. Finally, the original parapet and pediments fell in the 1886 earthquake and were not rebuilt accurately. Just as Mills's design of the Circular Church seems closely related to Latrobe's Baltimore Cathedral, so the Record Office seems indebted to Latrobe's Bank of Pennsylvania, 1799–1801. It was the first building in America to use vaults as an integral part of its architectural design, and, like the Record Office, it had round-headed windows set into recessed arches and pedimented porticoes dominating two façades.

In 1821 commissioners had been appointed by the legislature to select a site at or near Columbia for a State Lunatic Asylum. They were to study similar institutions in other states and report the number of insane people in South Carolina. In July, 1822, construction was begun on a building designed by Robert Mills. It was still incomplete in 1826, when the legislature was considering its sale or lease. In March, 1827, it was "yet in an unfinished state" but completed at last later that year.[22] Mills described the structure: "The design . . . combines elegance with permanence, economy and security from fire. The rooms are vaulted with brick, and the roof covered with copper. The building is large enough to accommodate upwards of 120 patients, besides furnishing spacious corridors, hospitals, refectories, a medical hall, several parlours, keepers' apartments, kitchens, and sundry offices. . . . The entrance to the centre building is under a grand portico of six massy Greek Doric columns, four feet in diameter, elevated on an open arcade . . . the whole surmounted by a pediment. . . . The plan, when completed, according to the original designs, will sweep a semicircle, or horse-shoe figure, and enclose a spacious court to the south."[23]

The main offices were entered from a two-story pedimented Greek Doric portico, raised on an arcaded basement. The basement contained kitchens, separate dining rooms for men and women and ten "cells for the refractory." The principal story contained family quarters for the staff, trustees' offices and an examining room. The attic contained hospitals for the men and women, a "Medical & Surgical Hall" and a copper-covered roof promenade for the sick and their visitors, made secure with a high parapet wall. The Asylum's plan recalls one of Latrobe's most important early works in America, the Virginia Penitentiary of 1797–98. The penitentiary was laid out as a semicircle of cells, three stories high, a single cell in depth, all facing an interior court. Similarly, Mills intended that the semicircle of cells at the Asylum would be closed with gardens for the inmates. Mills intended that the semicircular plan would be built in stages and saw completion of the central buildings by 1842. Samuel Sloan (1815–1884), a prolific Philadelphia designer of some thirty-two hospitals for the insane, added wings to the Asylum in 1883–84.[24]

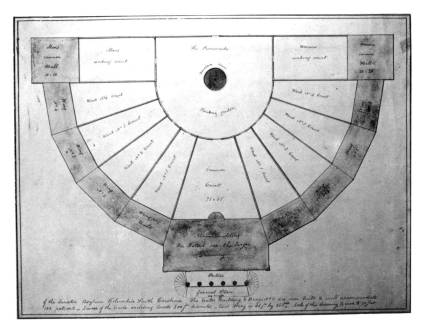

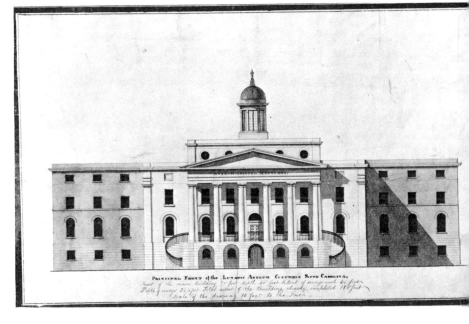

Lunatic Asylum, Columbia, 1822–26, plan for the principal building with wings and elevation, drawn by Robert Mills. *South Carolina Department of Archives and History*

In late 1822, Robert Mills designed a house in Columbia for Wade Hampton, planter, congressman and father of the famous South Carolina governor of the same name. Hampton planned to move into the city, because his wife had requested a house in town to escape from the warm weather fevers of rural Richland County. Judging from a surviving drawing, Hampton's house was planned around a central domed hall, loosely inspired by Palladian models. However, the project was

Wade Hampton House, Columbia,
drawing by Robert Mills, 1822.
South Carolina Historical Society

not built, because Hampton decided to purchase the house of Ainsley
Hall, a prosperous Columbia merchant who had come from England
twenty years earlier.

So now, in January, 1823, Ainsley Hall hired Mills to design a new
house for him.[25] The front façade of this two-story brick dwelling
recalls so many of Mills's public buildings, with its monumental pedimented portico supported by Roman Ionic columns and raised on an
arcaded ground story. This portico is flanked by two unusual windows:
conventional sashes, surmounted by semicircular wooden panels, are
recessed under a wide brick arch, a motif favored by Soane, Latrobe and
frequently used by Mills. The rear façade is shaded by a long, seven-bay
arcaded porch, and three-part windows light all the chambers on this
side. The parlors, located at the rear, are entered from the porch through
an apsidal recess, another motif which recalls Soane and Latrobe. In
plan, the hall and two parlors have ends which meet behind the recessed
entry from the porch, exactly the same arrangement designed twelve
years before for Senator Pope's house at Lexington, Kentucky, by Latrobe. Like Mills's design for Wade Hampton's house, Latrobe's design
for the Pope House had a central rotunda.

Construction of Ainsley Hall's house was begun in April, 1823, but
Hall died the following August. Work continued until June, 1825, but
the house was apparently still incomplete when it was sold "in this
present [unfinished] condition" to a theological seminary in 1829. Used
as an educational facility until 1963, the house was never used as a
residence, but the surviving specifications give some idea of the architect's intentions for the never-completed interior: "All the doors and

windows to be ... finished with double faced architraves or pilasters as may be directed. The doors to be dble work'd 2″ thick panneled. ... Inside shutters to fold in a box, front face panneled back flaps clamped secured with fastenings ... Dble torus moulded skirting on ground to all the rooms, passages & staircase. ... The stairs to be neatly & handsomely finished with a continuous rail of mahogany, & a scroll—balusters of curled maple or mahogany."[26] A kitchen, wood house, privy, smoke house, carriage house and gardener's house were planned. All have been destroyed, and the present flankers are inaccurate "reconstructions."

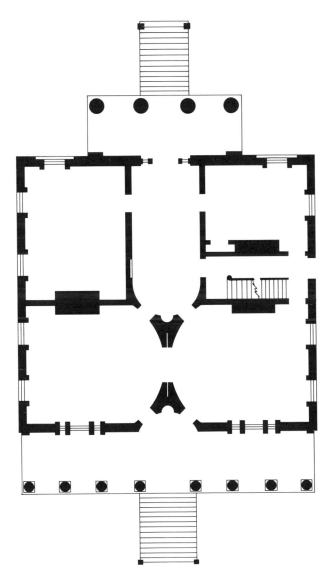

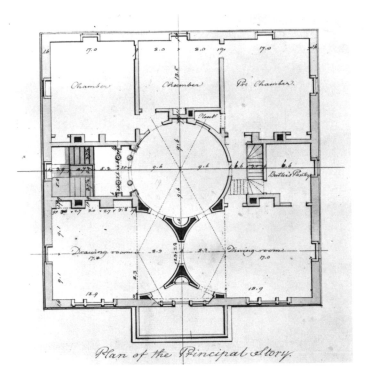

Ainsley Hall House, the plan of its principal floor, 1823, and possible model, Benjamin H. Latrobe's plan of Senator John Pope's House, Lexington, Kentucky, 1811. *Latrobe drawing: Library of Congress*

Plan of the Principal Story.

Ainsley Hall House,
Blanding Street, Columbia,
1823–29, views of front and
rear exteriors.

Ainsley Hall House, view of entrance from rear porch.

In 1824 construction of St. Peter's Catholic Church on Assembly Street in Columbia, designed by Robert Mills, was begun for a congregation established by Irish laborers who had come to South Carolina about 1821 to build public works. Mills's teacher Latrobe had designed the first Gothic Revival house in America, and now Mills designed the first Gothic Revival building in South Carolina. The plan of St. Peter's Church was a Greek cross, its length eighty feet and width, including transepts, sixty feet, with a tower of forty-five feet and above that a spire rising to an overall height of eighty feet. The exterior had corner buttresses, a lofty vaulted porch, a great circular window, a tower with battlements and flanking buttresses and finials. Inside, clustered columns supported side galleries and groin arches. Church records were burned in the Civil War, so we have only a description of the church from a contemporary newspaper: "You enter the Church by the vaulted porch . . . flanked on both sides by a flight of winding stone stairs leading to the galleries . . . and, passing through a spacious door with side lights and an arched transom, the first object that presents itself is the grand altar, which is placed in a spacious and lofty niche, thirty feet high, crowned by a semi-dome and lighted by a sky light."[27] The building was dedicated in December, 1830, enlarged in 1858 and demolished about 1908.

When Robert Mills wrote in 1827, "I have been engaged for the past six or seven years in the work of Internal Improvements in this state," he meant not only buildings, but public works of many kinds and books, too.[28] In 1821, he proposed "a great canal" which would connect Charleston and Columbia, and ultimately points further West, by means of an aqueduct bridge over the Congaree River.[29] It would, he promised, aid both transportation and irrigation. To carry out this visionary plan, a bill was introduced in the state legislature in December. The canal's route would have been surveyed, a list of landowners along the proposed route would have been assembled and the cost estimated, but the bill failed to pass. In 1822 Mills proposed a system of banking, draining and reclaiming river and swamp lands in the Carolina low country, so that region could be better cultivated and more healthful.[30] Mills sent a copy of his proposal to Jefferson in August, 1822.

Mills spent several years working on two books of lasting importance. *The Atlas of the State of South Carolina*, published at Baltimore in 1825, contains detailed maps of the state's twenty-eight districts, carefully corrected and annotated by the architect. Mills's *Statistics of South Carolina*, issued at Charleston in 1826, is a massive compendium of information about the state's history, geography, towns and villages,

St. Peter's Church, Columbia, 1824, early photograph before demolition.
Copy by Russell Maxey

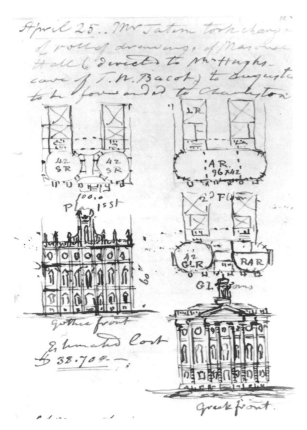

Masonic Hall, Charleston, sketches made by Robert Mills, 1828. *Tulane University Library*

lands and crops, lakes, creeks and streams, prices, climate, diseases, manufactures, fish, game, taxes, population, poor and eminent men, customs, amusements and miscellaneous observations.

In April, 1828, Mills prepared preliminary plans for a Masonic Hall in Charleston. He wrote in his diary on April 18th: "Made designs for Masonic Hall Charleston—100 ft front—45 feet deep main buildings with two wings in the rear each 70 feet by 27 ft whole . . . one Gothic and one Greek design."[31] The drawings sent to Charleston have been lost, but Mills made suggestive sketches of them in his diary. Again, Mills was following the example of Latrobe, who had made two plans, one Gothic and one classical, for the Baltimore Cathedral.

Mills returned to Baltimore in 1829 and then moved to Washington the following year, but his contributions to the architecture of his native state did not cease. In 1831 the United States government began construction of a new Marine Hospital at Charleston to care for sick and disabled seamen. Mills designed a two-story, hip-roofed structure with a T-shaped plan and double-tiered porches on an arcaded basement, Gothic clustered columns, flanking end pavilions and pointed arches. Plans and elevations for similar hospitals, designed in two versions for fifty and one hundred patients, were published at Washington in 1837, intended to be models for more marine hospitals in other ports. William G. Ramsay, physician in charge, described Charleston's Marine Hospital in 1836: "It is a commodious and airy building, fronting the west, and has double piazzas to the north, south and west, which are appropriated to the use of the patients. The front part of the building is occupied by the steward and his family. There are eight wards—three

Marine Hospital, Franklin Street, Charleston, 1831.

on the first floor, for surgical cases, and five on the second floor, one for venereal cases and four for medical cases."[32] Built by the Federal government, the Hospital was operated by the city. American sailors were admitted by the Collector of Customs, who paid the city sixty cents per day for each patient for up to four months' care. Foreign seamen could also be admitted by hospital administrators, when a ship's captain or foreign consul guaranteed payment of seventy-five cents per day. The Marine Hospital continued in operation until the Civil War, after which it was used, successively, as a freedmen's school, a library, orphanage and government offices.

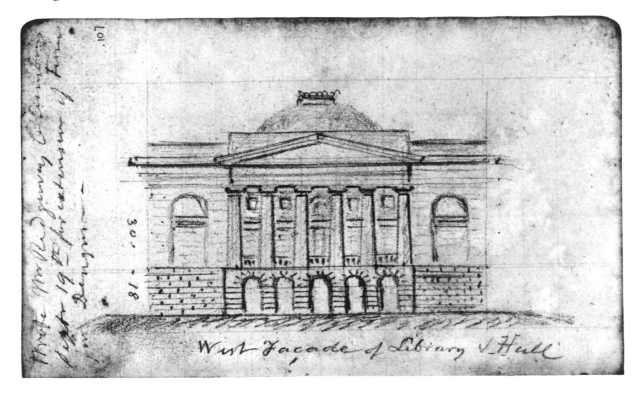

Library, University of South Carolina, sketch by Robert Mills, 1837. *Library of Congress*

In late 1836 the South Carolina College at Columbia was planning a new library, perhaps the first separate college library building in America. The name of the library's designer and the drawings have been lost. However, a surviving diary by Mills indicates that he was involved in its planning. One page in the diary bears the notation, "Wrote Mr. Ridgeway, Columbia, Septr. 19th for extension of time for Designs."[33] A nearby sketch, dated "January 27th 1837," pictures some elements incorporated into the finished building. Another Mills drawing, a more polished version of one of his plans, has been found at the Library itself. The Library, a three-story brick building with a central portico of four unfluted Doric columns, was completed in May, 1840. It was Mills's intention to locate the building at the end of the college quadrangle with a carriageway through the center of its basement story, turning the structure into a dramatic, heroic entrance to the College.

Library, University of South Carolina, Columbia, 1837–40. Left: Lithograph by Graham, c. 1850. *South Caroliniana Library, University of South Carolina*. Right: Photograph made before 20th century additions. *Library of Congress*

The completed interior of the Library resembles Bulfinch's original Library of Congress, designed in 1808 and burned in 1851. The Carolina Library's building contract, dated October, 1838, specifies that "alcoves and galleries . . . be precisely in the same manner as the congressional library at Washington."[34] Both the South Carolina College Library and the original Library of Congress had long, narrow reading rooms with alcoves, arcaded balcony and circular skylights. The Carolina building has a flat ceiling instead of the Washington Library's barrel-vaulted ceiling, but the ornamental plaster designs are almost identical. Mills, who had been appointed Federal Architect by President Jackson in 1836, would have been in an ideal position to send drawings from the national capital to South Carolina's capital. The Library was not built according to Mills's particular design and the similarities between it and the finished structure may be only coincidental, but it is noteworthy that Mills's last known contribution to the architecture of his native state was at the South Carolina College, where he had begun his career nearly forty years earlier.

In October, 1833, the South Carolina Railroad was opened between Charleston and the town of Hamburg, 136 miles, at the time the longest railroad in the world. Charleston's wharfs were covered with bales of cotton, boxes of fruit, bags of flour and crates of other goods. In 1848, Charleston's population had reached 26,451. A salt water bathing house, looking like a floating wooden temple, was built on piers extending into the Cooper River, and offered refreshments and band music. In March, 1848, gas was brought to Charleston, and the telegraph arrived six months later. The high battery, a great stone wall facing the harbor, was finally raised to its present height between the late 1830's and 1854, protecting the lowlying parts of the city from storms and floods. But sand in the streets was still so deep that carriages passed along "as noiselessly as gondolas in the canals of Venice."

The Greek Revival, which had become a national architectural style in America by the 1830's, was part of an artistic movement which swept across the entire Western world at the end of the 18th century and the start of the 19th century. James Stuart and Nicholas Revett had begun publication of their *Antiquities of Athens* in 1762. The monuments

VI.
The Greek Revival, 1830–1860

Charleston in the mid-19th century. Lithograph by Smith Brothers, 1851. *South Carolina Historical Society*

William Ravenal House, 13 East Battery, Charleston, 1835–45. Early photograph shows portico with Tower-of-the-Winds capitals before its collapse in 1886. *South Carolina Historical Society*

illustrated in their volumes—including the Monument of Lysicrates and the Tower of the Winds—became part of the 19th century's architectural vocabulary. The greatest Greek Revival house of South Carolina, Milford, built in 1839, used motifs borrowed from the Monument of Lysicrates, and at least three Charleston houses, dating from the late 1830's and 1840's, used variations of capitals from the Tower of the Winds. The Elgin Marbles had been brought from the Parthenon to England between 1803 and 1812. John Izard Middleton, born at Middleton Place in South Carolina, published a pioneering work of classical studies, *Greecian Remains in Italy . . . and Roman Antiquities*, in 1812.

The true Greek Revival came to America after the War of 1812, a cultural and economic watershed which enflamed American nationalism and discredited the Federalists, who had favored the dainty Adam style. Except for some buildings of Robert Mills, the new style came slowly to South Carolina.[1] Town market halls at Winnsboro, 1833, with its clock tower of 1837, Cheraw, 1836, and Georgetown, 1842, with its tower of 1845, are late Federal structures with Roman-inspired details. Philadelphia was the most fashionable city of America until the late 1820's, when the opening of the Erie Canal brought national preeminence to New York. The first important Greek Revival buildings were in Philadelphia, and, significantly, the first academically correct Greek Revival building in South Carolina, the Hibernian Hall at Charleston, was designed by a Philadelphian, Thomas U. Walter.

The Greek Revival has been explained as an expression of America's youthful democratic ideals. During the first half of the 19th century, fifteen states joined the Union, and, as the nation expanded, capitols, courthouses, city halls, churches, hospitals and hotels were, more often than not, built in the new Greek Revival style. In 1838 James Fenimore Cooper satirized the whims of fashion: "The public sentiment just now runs almost exclusively and popularly into the Greecian school. We build little besides temples for our churches and banks, our taverns, our courthouses, and our dwellings. A friend . . . has just built a brewery on the model of the Temple of the Winds!"[2] Cooper was as accurate as witty, for two of the most beautiful early Greek Revival buildings of Charleston were commissioned for an Irish fraternal society and an ancient Jewish congregation! A Greek Revival storefront was installed at 186 King Street, Charleston, by Andrew Moffit about 1849.

Unlike painters, who could visit galleries in European capitals to see the great masters, architects were seldom able to see firsthand the great buildings of the past. And, in any case, most buildings were still produced by carpenters who looked to books for their models. Greek details first appeared in American books with John Haviland's *The Builder's Assistant*, published at Philadelphia in 1818. The more old-fashioned Massachusetts housewright Asher Benjamin did not include Greek details in his books until the sixth edition of *The American Builder's Companion* in 1827. Three years later, in his *Practical House Carpenter*, Benjamin wrote: "Since my last publication, the Roman School of architecture has been entirely changed for the Greecian." The most influential handbooks which spread the Greek Revival in America were Benjamin's *The Practical House Carpenter*, Minard Lafever's *Modern Builder's Guide*, 1833, and Lafever's *Beauties of Modern Architecture*, 1835. The doorway of the Charles Kerrison House, 1842, at 138 Wentworth Street, Charleston, is taken from plate 63 of Lafever's *Modern Builder's Guide*. Its portico is based on the ubiquitous Tower of the Winds.

Doorway of the Charles Kerrison House, 138 Wentworth Street, Charleston, 1842, with its model, plate 63 of Minard Lafever's *Modern Builder's Guide* (New York, 1833). *Lafever illustration: Charleston Library Society*

Samuel Y. Tupper House, 24 Ann Street, Charleston, c. 1835, stair and doorway. *Carolina Art Association*

Except for the application of Greek details, houses of the Greek Revival period differed little from Federal dwellings. Columns and porticoes could suggest ancient grandeur, whether they were correct classical architecture or not. Side halls and twin parlors became the most common city plan, and oval rooms went out of fashion. Interiors were decorated with simple, heavy Doric pilasters and entablatures, sometimes enriched with Greek motifs, around doors and windows and fireplaces. Walls were generally plain plaster with heavier cornices and higher baseboards, often painted to imitate marble. Stairs now had more massive balusters and newels. Doorways had long rectangular transoms in place of elliptical and semicircular fanlights favored during the Federal period.

Robert Mills's Public Record Office, 1822, the first Greek Revival building in South Carolina, came far ahead of the general tide of fashion. It was really ten years later that rich Charlestonians began to adopt the new style, and even then only by adding Greek details to older dwellings. Between 1831 and 1834, Elias Horry made changes to the house at 59 Meeting Street, which had been built in the mid-18th century by William Branford. Horry added wide hall doorways with Greek Revival details on the inside and two-tiered porches to the front and rear exteriors. Though not Greek in detail, these porches reflect the vogue for things classical. Similarly, Greek Revival porches were added later to the Robert Primrose House at 332 East Bay Street, 1817, a typical Federal style house with elliptical fanlights and dainty sidelights. During the 1830's several transitional houses, combining Federal and Greek Revival details, were built in Charleston. Robert Martin's house at 16 Charlotte Street, built between 1834 and 1840, Samuel Y. Tupper's house at 24 Ann Street, built about 1835, and Elias Vanderhorst's house at 28 Chapel Street, built after 1832, all have Greek Revival porches which are approached by pairs of circular stairs and lead to doorways with elliptical fanlights.

Between 1833 and 1836 William Aiken, Jr., Governor of South Carolina between 1844 and 1846, remodeled a house at 48 Elizabeth Street which he had inherited from his father two years before. The house had been built in 1818 by John Robinson, who sold it to William Aiken, Sr., in 1825. Now the younger Aiken remodeled the interior of a fairly typical late Federal house, added a dining room and connected it to the rear of the old house with a dramatic new Greek Revival entrance hall. There, under a groin-vaulted ceiling, a pair of stone steps with cast-iron railings ascend against the opposite sides of the hall to a landing, which is supported by fluted Doric columns, while a short central flight of

John Robinson/William Aiken, Jr. House, 48 Elizabeth Street, Charleston, entrance hall added 1833–36.

William Bradford/Elias Horry House, 59 Meeting Street, Charleston,
an 18th century house to which a portico was added 1831–34.

Robert Primrose House, 332 East Bay Street, a house of c. 1817 to which a piazza was added, probably in late 1830's.

Edmonston-Alston House, parlor.

steps descends to the basement. In 1857–58, Aiken added another wing—a skylit, octagonal art gallery—on the northwest side of the house.

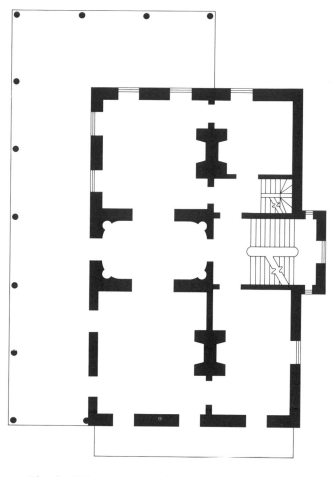

Charles Edmonston/William Alston House, 21 East Battery, Charleston, a house of 1829 enlarged after 1837.

After the Panic of 1837, Charles Edmondston, a Scottish immigrant who had made and lost a fortune in shipping, sold his house at 21 East Battery, originally built in 1829, to William Alston, who gave it to his son Charles. Charles rebuilt the piazza in more imposing Greek Revival grandeur, replaced the elliptical fanlight with a squarish, trabeated doorway and hid the old hipped roof behind a new parapet wall. It is not known exactly what changes were made to the interiors.

In 1835 Charleston's Hibernian Society, a social and charitable organization founded in 1799 by Irishmen to aid their fellow immigrants, advertised in the newspapers of Boston, New York, Philadelphia, Baltimore and Washington for "the chastest models of Greecian and Roman architecture" to build a new hall. The design of Thomas U. Walter of Philadelphia was selected.[3] Walter (1804–1887) was the son of a bricklayer and stonemason and a student of William Strickland. The building committee, in its final report, acknowledged that the Greek Revival was new and unfamiliar when it complained of the difficulties of executing Walter's design "from the novelty it presents to us and the consequent absence of materials and want of capable artists."[4] Significantly, Hibernian Hall had been designed by an architect from style-setting Philadelphia, where the Greek Revival had first established itself in America some twenty years earlier.

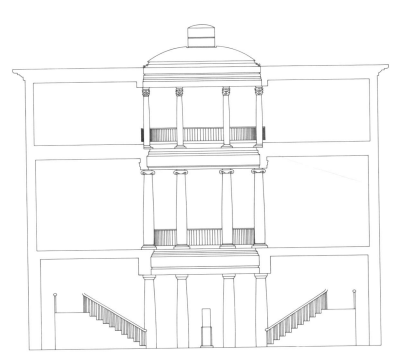

Hibernian Society Hall, 105 Meeting Street, Charleston, 1839–40. Photograph shows appearance of the building before its portico collapsed in 1886. *South Carolina Historical Society*

Construction of Hibernian Hall was delayed because of a terrible fire in April, 1838, but the cornerstone was finally laid in March, 1839. In May, a portion of the partially completed brick façade collapsed. As the bricks fell, carrying away the scaffolding on which they were standing, the workmen grabbed at projecting rafters and clambered up to safety on the roof.[5] The Hall was opened at last in January, 1840.[6] An extraordinary cylindrical stair hall, surrounded by circular balconies, rises three stories to a coffered dome with oculus. When the original portico collapsed in the 1886 earthquake, it was replaced by one with modillion cornice and a round-headed window in the pediment.

Charles F. Reichardt, an architect who worked in New York as early as 1835 and who was one of the eleven founding members of the American Institution of Architects, came to Charleston in December, 1836. The Charleston *Mercury* of January 12, 1837, reported: "We understand that the plan for the New Hotel by Mr. Reichardt having been chosen, a contract was made . . . for its immediate execution."[7] By the end of March, 1838, Reichardt's Charleston Hotel was virtually

Hibernian Society Hall, interior.

complete, and a celebratory dinner was held there for investors and their friends. Suddenly the new hotel became one of several hundred buildings destroyed by the calamitous fire of 1838. By June, rebuilding was already underway on the surviving foundations, and the new Charleston Hotel was completed in November, 1839. The hotel, called "this mammoth caravansera" at the time, was a four-story brick structure, finished with stucco and built around a central court.[8] A splendid portico of fourteen colossal Corinthian columns, raised on a loggia which served as a base for the design and decorated with acroteria on its pediment, extended 150 feet along Meeting Street. This design recalls the similar long, raised Corinthian portico at LaGrange Terrace, 1832–36, by Town and Davis, which Reichardt would certainly have seen while he was in New York. The dining room floor of the new hotel was painted to resemble oak, and its interior court was soon laid out in walks and grass.[9] William Ferguson stayed at the Hotel in 1855 and, when put into a room with three beds, and perhaps more guests, he complained: "Americans seem, in travelling, to prefer clubbing together as much as possible, in one bed room or even in one bed!"[10] Suprisingly, this great monument of the Greek Revival was demolished in 1960. Reichardt also designed a theater, a steeple for Robert Mills's Circular Church and a guardhouse before leaving Charleston about 1841.

Charleston Hotel, Meeting Street, Charleston, 1837–39. Lithograph by Thayer and Company, c. 1845. *Carolina Art Association*

Charleston Hotel, photographed in 1865. *Library of Congress*

Milford, Pinewood vicinity, 1839–41. *Library of Congress*

Milford was built in 1839–41 outside the hamlet of Pinewood as the country residence of John L. Manning, Governor of South Carolina between 1852 and 1854 and the richest delegate to South Carolina's secession convention in 1860 with more than six hundred slaves and more than $2 million in property. Even before glimpsing, through shadowy, moss-hung trees, its great portico glistening in the sun at the top of a distant hillside, a visitor knows that Milford will be something special, when he passes a small Greek Ionic temple serving as a jewel-like porter's lodge. The three-story main house, its façade dominated by a monumental portico of six stop-fluted Corinthian columns, is connected by quadrant passageways to matching dependencies, a kitchen and laundry. Attic windows are hidden in wreaths which ornament the entablature on each side of the house. A spring house, designed as a miniature Gothic cathedral, sits in a shaded hollow to the west of the residence.

The scale and richness of Milford's interior equals the grandeur of its exterior. Architraves of doors are embellished with lively details copied from Minard Lafever's *Beauties of Modern Architecture*, published in New York in 1835. A circular stair is set beneath a ribbed dome with oculus. Nine-foot high mahogany doors are fitted with silver-plated locks and hinges. The double parlors are divided by two screens of Corinthian columns in antis. Mirrored panels, hinged against the side walls between the columns, can be closed to divide the rooms or opened to make one hall for festivities, a design also found, along with that of the parlor centerpieces, in Lafever's book. Front and rear windows are engineered so that all sashes can be pushed through the tops of their frames, providing unrestricted access to porches.

Several personalities were involved in the design of Milford. Governor Manning, himself, participated in the design. A drawing for entrance gates seems to be in his hand. In September, 1839, he proposed substituting two matching dependencies in place of the single kitchen which had been planned and made sketches showing how they might be positioned.[11] Construction was supervised by Nathaniel F. Potter (1807–1874) of Providence, Rhode Island, where he was listed in city directories between 1830 and 1840 as a brickmason. Potter had come to Charleston in June, 1838, to supervise rebuilding of the Charleston Hotel. The columns and capitals of Milford's monumental portico recall those of the hotel. In May, 1839, Potter was recommended to Manning by William Gregg, a South Carolina merchant who would become famous as founder of the Graniteville Company in the 1840's. At Milford, Potter made many modifications to the plans which he had probably drawn in consultation with the owner. But in November,

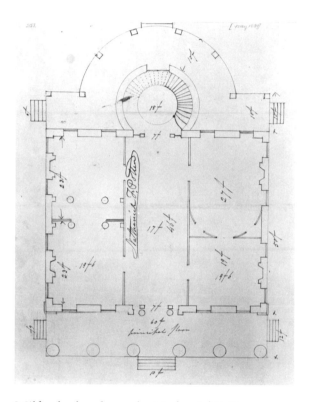

Milford, plan drawn by Nathaniel F. Potter. *South Caroliniana Library, University of South Carolina*

1839, Manning paid "M. Warren's Bill for Drawing, $10.00" and in November, 1840, "Major Warren's Bill for Plans, outbuildings" was also paid.[12] Russell Warren of Providence had spent winters in Charleston, where he owned property and was listed in the 1821 city directory as "carpenter." Warren must have been called in to make drawings of some details. Finally, on May 12, 1839, Potter wrote to Manning, "I Shall want to send to N York to have you A regular Set of drawings made,"[13] which suggests that another draftsman in New York was also involved. Between August, 1835, and August, 1836, Warren had worked for A. J. Davis in New York.

Fortunately, this greatest of all Greek Revival houses in South Carolina is also one of the best documented. Articles of agreement between Manning and Potter were signed on May 7, 1839. Potter sent plans and specifications to Manning on May 12: "Collonade to be composed of six Corinthian columns, the style to be used is that from the monument of Lysicratus, the Bases of the columns to be of granite, the shafts of bricks & the capitals of Wood. . . . The whole exterior of the house to be plastered, all the collums & mouldings with cement, & the balance with rough cast, the whole body of the House to be straw colored and all the trimmings white. . . . There is to be frieze lights to light & ventilate the attic. . . . The drawing room to be finished with sliding and folding doors (as per plate No. 7 in Lafevers modern Architecture 1835). . . . . All the doors and windows in the hall and dining room & Library to be finished

Centerpiece at Milford, with its model, plate 21 of Minard Lafever's *Beauties of Modern Architecture* (New York, 1835). *Lafever illustration: Avery Library, Columbia University*

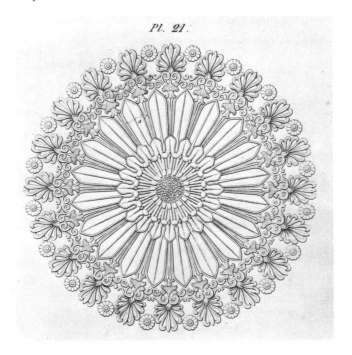

Milford, parlors.

Milford, stairhall.

Doorway at Milford, with its model, plate 19 of Minard Lafever's *Beauties of Modern Architecture* (New York, 1835). *Lafever illustration: Avery Library, Columbia University*

as per plate 19 in Lafever. . . . . All the doors of the second story to be finished as pr plate no 14 with no 19 cornice. . . . . Front entrance to be as p/ plate no 13. . . . All the above plates refered to are from Lafever's Modern Architecture of 1835." On August 2, Potter wrote: "The drawings for your house is at last finished." Work was to begin on November 1. Lumber and bricks were made locally. Machines were purchased for brickmaking, and four sawyers were hired from Charleston. Hardware, lead pipe and mirrors came from New York. Mantels were supplied by John Struthers of Philadelphia, the first of them shipped in mid-March, 1840. The final bill was rendered in May, 1841.[14]

When William Roper built his new house at 9 East Battery in Charleston in 1838, on land recently filled in behind the new walls of the high battery, it was the southernmost dwelling facing the Cooper River. Taking advantage of this wonderful site, with its splendid views of the harbor, an anonymous designer enlarged the typical Charleston side piazza into an heroically scaled monumental Greek Ionic colonnade, overlooking the entire tip of the peninsula. It is a good demonstration of how a persistent local house type could be adapted to new fashions in architecture.

William Roper House, 13 East Battery, Charleston, 1838. *Library of Congress*

When the old Beth Elohim Synagogue, 74 Hasell Street, burned in April, 1838, the congregation began to plan a new building.[15] In November, Charles F. Reichardt was paid $100 for "a plan of the Exterior & Interior of the Synagogue." Plans were also submitted by James Curtis, David Lopez and Frederick Wesner, three local builders. In April, 1839, the congregation accepted a plan "with the Greecian & Doric portico" of Charles B. Tappan and George W. Noble, builders listed in the 1840–41 city directory. In May, the building committee was advised by "Mr. Potter, the builder of the New Hotel" that construction should not proceed without more detailed working drawings. Then either Potter or David Lopez sent the original drawings, which had been "framed & stretched on canvass in order to preserve them, as they would otherwise break and be unfit for use," to New York. There Cyrus L. Warner, who was probably a draftsman or journeyman printer, enlarged them into detailed plans and specifications, which were sent to Charleston in July.

Beth Elohim Synagogue, 74 Hassell Street, Charleston, 1840–41, exterior view.

Beth Elohim Synagogue, interior.

The building contract, signed in October, 1839, has survived.[16] The floor of the portico was to be paved with dark blue or black and white marble tiles, laid on brick arches. The columns of the portico were to be "work'd in the brick work." The visible foundation, window and door sills, lintels, steps, column capitals and bases and the architrave of the portico were to be of blue granite. The walls, partitions and ceilings were "to be lath'd with saw'd laths four feet long to be put up with five nails to the lath." Foundation walls were to be local brick, but the pediments, columns, cornices, triglyphs and window architraves were to be "best northern well burn'd bricks." Finally, there was to be no work done on the premises on the Sabbath or festival days. The cornerstone was laid in January, 1840, and the building was dedicated in March, 1841.[17] The original interior had benches parallel to the sidewalls, a gallery for women around three sides and a reading platform in the center. Alterations were made in 1879 and 1886, but the interior retains a dramatic shallow dome and handsome tabernacle.

In Charleston, and elsewhere in South Carolina, other Greek temples were soon begun. In 1842 the Second Baptist Church, now the Centenary Methodist Church, was built at 60 Wentworth Street. When the building committee insisted on small doors behind the columns of the portico, an arrangement incorrect in classical architecture, the designer, Edward Brickell White, overruled and overwrought, declined to superintend construction.[18] The courthouse at Camden, which Robert Mills had designed in 1825, was remodeled in 1847, its original Roman Ionic columns replaced by a complete Greek Doric portico. The courthouse at Newberry, designed by Jacob Graves, was begun in the fall of 1850 and completed in 1853. The courthouse at Abbeville, another Greek temple, was built in 1852. In Charleston, the Bethel Methodist Church was built at 57 Pitt Street between 1852 and 1853. James M. Curtis was the builder and possible designer. The Salem Black River Presbyterian Church was built near Mayesville in 1846, a two-story brick temple with Doric portico and antae, designed by J. Lomas of Columbia, who probably intended to stucco its exterior.

In the late 1820's Carolina builders had expressed their classical leanings by adding Roman porticoes to older buildings. Throughout the Greek Revival period, many builders combined Roman and Greek details, probably because of the lasting traditions of Georgian building and the strong influence of Jeffersonian classicism transmitted through the example of Robert Mills. Mills seems to have almost always confused Greek and Roman details in his writings and combined them casually in his buildings. In a world of few trained designers, local

Bethel Methodist Church, 57 Pitt Street, Charleston, 1852–53. *South Carolina Historical Society*

Above: Courthouse, Camden, 1825, remodeled 1847. Below: Courthouse, Newberry, 1850–53.

Above: Second Baptist Church, 60 Wentworth Street, Charleston, 1842. Below: Salem Black River Presbyterian Church, Mayesville vicinity, 1846.

Market Hall, 188 Meeting Street, Charleston, 1840. *Library of Congress*

housewrights inevitably copied familiar patterns, selecting details without academic exactitude.

The designs of Charleston's Edward Brickell White often combined Greek and Roman details. White was born in St. John's Parish of South Carolina in 1806, the son of an artist. He studied engineering at West Point, where he graduated in 1826. After serving as an artillery officer, he resigned from the Army in 1836. At first employed as railroad surveyor and builder and as Inspector of the Boilers and Machinery of Steam Boats in Charleston in late 1838, White devoted himself primarily to architecture after 1839.[19]

In 1840 White designed the Market Hall at 188 Meeting Street in Charleston, replacing an older market which had burned in 1838. Modeled on the Temple of Fortuna Virilis at Rome, the market stands on a rusticated base with an open arcade, and is stuccoed except for its sandstone trim. Double flights of stone steps with wrought and cast-iron railings lead up to a pedimented Roman Doric portico. The elaborate entablature includes bucrania, rams' skulls and triglyphs. The mouldings of the Doric capitals and bases have been extended along the side and rear walls. Wood-roofed brick stalls for produce-sellers stretched behind the market toward the river, where, close to their boats, fish-mongers sold their catch.

In 1850, White, a trustee of the College of Charleston, designed wings and Roman Ionic portico for its main building, which had been built in 1828–29 to the plans of William Strickland. In 1852 White also designed a porter's lodge and an iron railing around the campus.

In March, 1850, White exhibited a model and drawing of his design for the proposed new Custom House.[20] It was to be three stories high, 300 feet wide, 200 feet deep, eighty feet high, with a cupola rising one hundred feet above the roof. Though plans of another architect, Ammi B. Young, were finally selected, White was made supervising architect of the project. Young (1800–1874) was born in New Hampshire, son of a builder and architect. He worked in Vermont and Massachusetts in the 1830's and 1840's and succeeded Robert Mills as supervisor of Federal buildings at Washington in 1851. In July, 1851, White was in Baltimore, heading further North if necessary, to locate the machinery for setting foundation pilings of the new Custom House.

Progress was slow. In 1856 the Treasury Department complained that "The new custom-house . . . has not advanced as rapidly as could have been desired. . . . The superintendent attributes this to the delay in receiving the granite and marble."[21] In 1859 the Congress refused to appropriate more funds for construction, and in 1861 White was re-

United States Custom House, East Bay Street, Charleston, begun 1850, seen during construction after the Civil War. *Library of Congress*

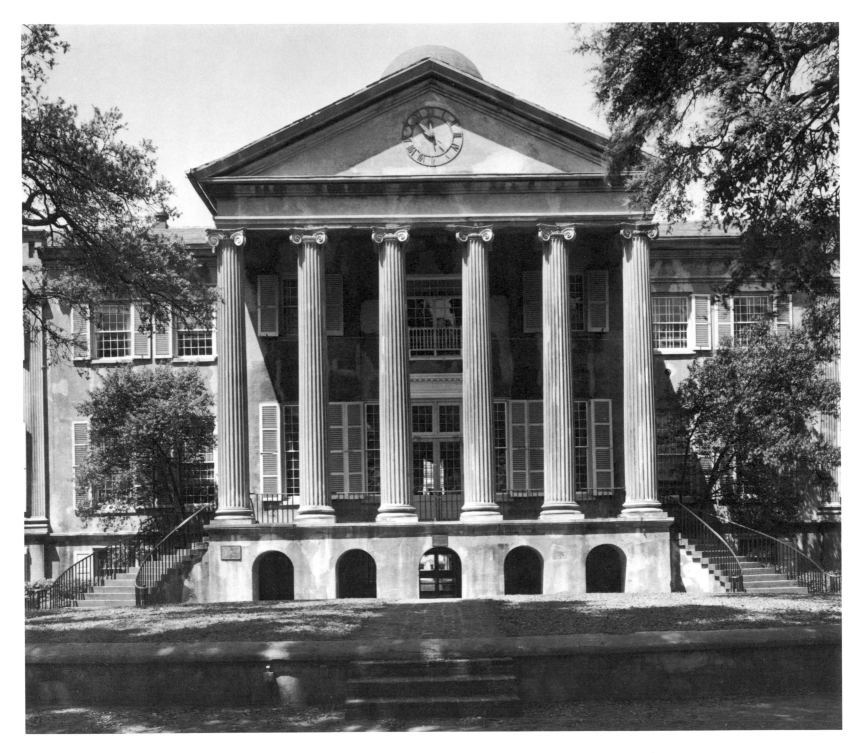

College of Charleston, 66 George Street, Charleston, portico and wings added in 1850 to a building constructed in 1828.

portedly aiding the Confederates at their forts when he should have been on the job at the Custom House. Construction proceeded fitfully after the Civil War and was finally completed, without Young's dome and side porticoes, in 1879.

Edward C. Jones was another designer of the period whose buildings combined Greek and Roman details. He was born in July, 1822, the son of a Charleston custom office employee. In 1838, at the age of sixteen, he determined to become an architect. Apprenticed to builder James Curtis, he studied drawing for "a month or two" with a Professor Guthrie, his only formal architectural training. He then worked for David Lopez, builder of the Beth Elohim Synagogue, who gave him a copy of Stuart and Revett's *Antiquities of Athens*.[22] He designed the Westminster Presbyterian Church, now the Trinity Methodist Church, at 275 Meeting Street, Charleston, in 1848. Its portico is Roman, but much of its interior decoration is Greek. The new chapel at the South Carolina College, designed by Jacob Graves in 1852, is a similar giant prostyle temple, more Roman than Greek.

Left: Westminster Presbyterian Church, 275 Meeting Street, Charleston, 1848. Right: Chapel, University of South Carolina, 1852. *Photograph of the University Chapel: South Carolina Historical Society*

Of the Greek orders, the Doric was the most favored by American builders, because it was the simplest and therefore the cheapest to build. No matter how academically incorrect, a few columns on a front porch would suggest the classical world. The carpenter could create a more convincing temple-like house by placing a columned portico, with a

Westminster Presbyterian Church, interior.

pediment running from a low-pitched gable roof, on the short side of a conventional house. Or the builder could simulate the appearance of a peripteral temple by running a peristyle portico around all four sides of a conventional house.

In the town of Beaufort, several early houses were remodeled in the Greek Revival period. Milton Maxey's house at 1113 Craven Street was partially demolished by a later owner, Edmund Rhett, after 1830 and a two-story frame structure, with two-tiered Greek Revival porch, was erected over the tabby basement walls of the original house. In the 1840's Thomas Rhett added another two-tiered porch to the front of a nearby house built by an unidentified owner about 1820. A dainty, old-fashioned Venetian window can still be seen behind the massive Greek Revival porch, and the interiors retain their Adamesque plaster decoration and panelled dado from the Federal era. Finally, Dr. George Stoney's house at 500 Port Republic Street, built about 1823, was remodeled with Greek Revival porches in the 1840's.

Thomas Badgett built a one-and-one-half story cottage at Laurens sometime before 1846. A carefully detailed entablature, with triglyphs and metopes, runs around three sides of the building, with pilasters at the angles. Unusual three-part windows with glazed transoms contribute to the interest of this elegant but sadly neglected building. There is evidence that porches, now removed, once stood at both sides of the house. Door and windows are copied from Plate 28 of Asher Benjamin's *The Practice of Architecture* of 1833. James Alexander Pettigrew built another Greek Revival cottage, Bonnie Shade, about 1854 in Florence for his daughter and her husband, Joseph F. Wingate. Cool Springs, a two-and-one-half story frame structure with a two-tiered porch, was built in Camden in 1832 for John Boykin and enlarged in 1853 for James B. Cureton by builder Reuben Hamilton. Magnolia, a two-story frame house on a tall elevated brick basement, with a monumental Greek Doric portico extending across its entire front, was built at Eastover in 1855.

In the country, a housewright might substitute square pillars for properly tapered Greek columns, an economy often practiced in the 1850's. An undocumented two-story frame house, located on the road between Johnston and Edgefield, has a handsome pedimented portico with square pillars. It is a simple farmhouse, but a clever builder adjusted the spacing of his second-story windows to accommodate the high pediment of the one-story portico. Three separate front doors lead into the central hall and the two rooms on either side of it. The interior—floors, ceilings and walls—is completely sheathed with flush boards.

Plate 28 of Asher Benjamin's *The Practice of Architecture* (Boston, 1833), the model for door and window frames at Thomas Badgett House, Laurens. *Private Collection*

Above: Thomas Badgett House, Laurens, before 1846. Below: Magnolia, Eastover, 1855.

Above: Milton Maxey/Edmund Rhett House, 1113 Craven Street, Beaufort, an early house remodeled after 1830. Below: Lewis Reeve Sams House, 601 Bay Street, Beaufort, 1852.

Undocumented House, Edgefield County, c. 1850.

Camp Hill, Glenn Springs, 1835, enlarged c. 1850.

Orange Grove, Anderson, 1840–42, enlarged c. 1850. *Library of Congress*

Black Mingo Baptist Church, interior view.

Camp Hill, two miles south of Glenn Springs, was built about 1835 for Dr. Winn Smith, originally a simple up-country farmhouse with board ceilings, walls of flush vertical boards over panelled wainscotting and wooden mantels with carved sunbursts. About 1850 two wings, a doctor's office and plantation office, were added, connected to the old farmhouse by long porches with square pillars. In 1882 a pediment was added to the central portion of this porch and the tympanum was filled with the fishscale shingles so popular in that era. Orange Grove in Anderson was built in 1840–42, a two-story frame house on low brick basement. About 1850 wings were added, linked to the old house by a long porch with simplified Doric pillars.

A Greek Revival exterior and Roman interior are combined at Black Mingo Baptist Church at Nesmith, built in 1843. Inside, there is a barrel-vaulted ceiling and long galleries supported by slender Tuscan columns. The walls are finished with vertical flush boards above the chair rail and horizontal flush boards below it. An inscription over the front door reads: "Come unto me, all ye that labour & are heavy laden & I will give you rest." Throughout the interior there are affectingly personal quotations from scripture. On the pulpit: "And he said unto them, Go ye into all the world and preach the gospel to every creature." On a frieze under the gallery: "When ye stand praying, forgive, if ye have aught against any, that your Father also which is in heaven may forgive you your trespasses." On a golden sunburst tablet at the back of the barrel-vaulted ceiling: "Let your light so shine before men, that they may see your good works and glorify your Father which is in Heaven."

Black Mingo Baptist Church, Nesmith, 1843.

VII.
Romantic Styles,
1840–1863

By the late 1840's, despite railroads and cotton, South Carolina was beginning to suffer economic difficulties, which were reflected in the diminished quality and variety of the state's buildings. Early efforts at manufacturing had been made at the end of the 18th century—a nail and hoe-making factory and Benjamin Waring's cotton factory at Stateburg, the Boatwright waterpowered cotton gins at Columbia, Hill and Hayne's iron furnace and nail factory in York, the Hill brothers' ironworks at Spartanburg, Abner Landrum's stoneware factory outside Edgefield.[2] Enterprises like these were at first encouraged by the restrictions on commerce which preceded the War of 1812, but then collapsed after the resumption of trade—and foreign imports—when peace was restored. A small arms manufactory at Andersonville produced only one hundred guns before closing, and David Williams's cotton factory at Cedar Creek, near Society Hill, closed in the 1820's. Except for cotton mills at Spartanburg and Greenville, manufacturing in South Carolina had declined by the 1820's, when hostility toward the tariff began to be reflected in hostility to industry.

South Carolina became a land devoted to cotton, rice and slaves. In 1802, the state had reopened the interstate slave trade, which had been ended in 1792, and in 1804 it resumed the foreign slave trade, which had been prohibited in 1787. A manual farm economy, based on two important cash crops and slave labor, had a natural limit to its productivity. Virgin lands were settled, rapidly exhausted and inevitably abandoned. South Carolina and the older southeastern states were now eclipsed by boom times in the Southwest. In 1820 South Carolina had produced more cotton than any other state, but by 1840 its production was exceeded by that of Georgia, Alabama, Mississippi and Louisiana. Customs duties at Charleston declined from a yearly average of $1,400,000 in the 1815–18 period to $505,000 in 1831.

By about 1830 the tide of white immigration into South Carolina had ended and people even began to leave.[3] The eighth most populous state in 1820, South Carolina was only the fourteenth most populous by 1850. Nearly half of the white people born in South Carolina after 1800 left the state between 1820 and 1860. In 1860, of the 470,257 whites born in South Carolina who lived in the United States, 193,389 had left their native state. Though the general shifting of population was everywhere toward the West, South Carolina's exodus rate was still twice as high as the other states. Meanwhile, South Carolina was not attracting new immigrants. In 1860 more than 90% of the people living in the state had been born there. Newcomers with new ideas, bold Barbadian planters and ambitious Englishmen, had enriched the life and building of colonial Carolina. New Englanders had made an important, though generally overlooked, contribution to life in South Carolina during the first forty years after the Revolution, especially in business and education.

Gothic ornament had been one of several exotic decorative styles used in 18th century England. Designers set out to delight the eye and spirit with garden follies, special rooms and sometimes, though rarely, entire houses built in some ancient, medieval or oriental style. Batty Langley's *Gothic Architecture Improved*, 1742, and William and John Halfpenny's *Chinese and Gothic Architecture Properly Ornamented*, 1752, showed builders how to add these fanciful touches to the old symmetrical, geometric, classical buildings of the time. In 18th century Charles Town, Gothic decorations appear on one of the sumptuous marble mantels at the Miles Brewton House. Charleston bookseller Robert Wells sold Paul Decker's *Chinese Architecture, Civil and Ornamental*, published in London in 1755. John Lord, "Carver and Gilder from London" who was active in Charles Town between 1766 and 1773, produced "console brackets, ionic, corinthian and composite Capitals, trusses, mouldings of various different patterns, with every kind of ornament proper for decorating the insides of rooms, in the French, Chinese and Gothic taste."[1] Benjamin Latrobe brought the idea of dressing traditional buildings in exotic costumes when he came to America in 1796, and his South Carolina pupil Robert Mills designed at least three efforts in the Gothic style: St. Peter's Church at Columbia, 1824, unexecuted studies for a Masonic Hall at Charleston, 1828, and the Marine Hospital, Charleston, 1831. In 19th century Charleston, Gothic Revival outbuildings, privies and stables were often built behind older houses.

In the 1830's and 1840's, a new kind of Gothic Revival began to make its way from England to America. Scotland's Sir Walter Scott portrayed scenes of heroic medieval pagentry in his novels, popularizing the Gothic world. He built himself a Gothic castle, inspiring copies in America. A reflection of the Romantic movement in all of Western culture, Gothic buildings were intended to be private, personal, sentimental and a little bit quirky. A gesture of escape from the growing complexity, urbanization and industrialization of modern life, Romantic cottages and villas were designed for rural and suburban settings. Influenced by the vast American landscape, which had so powerful an impact on painting and literature, Romantic architecture was intended to spring naturally, organically, sympathetically from its pastoral surroundings. Significantly, the Gothic Revival in America first flourished

Above: Sunnyside, 105 Dargan Street, Greenwood, c. 1851. Below: Arsenal, Beaufort, early 19th century structure remodeled in Gothic style in mid-century. *South Carolina Historical Society*

in the Hudson River Valley of New York, a center of landscape painting in the early 19th century. A Gothic cottage called Sunnyside, evidently inspired by Washington Irving's home of the same name on the Hudson, was built by farmer Robert C. Gillam at Greenwood, South Carolina, about 1851.

It is also significant that the greatest creator and popularizer of the Gothic Revival came from the city of New York, which had burgeoned after the completion of the Erie Canal in 1827, and not from Philadelphia, which had led the acceptance of Greek Revival building a generation earlier. New York's Alexander Jackson Davis designed his first Gothic house in the early 1830's. He had begun his career as an architectural illustrator. His fame and influence came not only from his commissions but from his drawings, which were used by Andrew Jackson Downing, horticulturalist and architectural theorist, in three important works, *A Treatise on the Theory and Practice of Landscape Gardening*, 1841, *Cottage Residences*, 1842, and *Architecture of Country Houses*, 1850. A Gothic cottage at Barnwell, South Carolina, perhaps intended as the rectory of the nearby Church of the Holy Apostles, was built about 1848 and seems clearly modeled on the illustrations in Downing's books.

In these works, the formal, symmetrical, mostly white houses of the neoclassic period were replaced by informal, asymmetrical, earth-colored villas of the Romantic era. Roofs became steeply-pitched gables, with extended eaves and decorated bargeboards. Rooflines were further enlivened with clustered tall chimney stacks, towers, crenelled parapets, finials and crocket ornaments. Board-and-batten siding—boards laid vertically, their joints covered with thin slats or battens—emphasized the verticality of the Gothic style. Façades were complicated with trellised verandahs, clustered columns, bay and oriel windows, Tudor, ogee or pointed arches, stone tracery and corner buttresses with weatherings. Interiors were decorated with plaster vaults, leaded stained glass, drip mouldings and foliated ornament.

Though the Gothic Revival was in part a reaction to industrialization, elaborate Gothic ornament was facilitated by steam-powered saw mills and iron foundries. Perhaps the region's industrial backwardness was one reason why the Gothic Revival was used less often in the South than in the North and Midwest. In South Carolina, with hardly a handful of known exceptions, the Gothic Revival was used exclusively for churches, military buildings and jails. Because of its association with the great cathedrals of the Middle Ages, Gothic architecture was often used for ecclesiastical building.

Undocumented cottage, Barnwell, c. 1848.

Huguenot Church, 136 Church Street, Charleston, 1844–45. *Carolina Art Association*

Edward Brickell White was born in St. John's Parish of South Carolina in 1806. He studied engineering at West Point and graduated in 1826. After serving as an artillery officer, he resigned from the Army in 1836. At first employed as railroad surveyor and builder and as Inspector of the Boilers and Machinery of Steam Boats in Charleston in late 1838, White devoted himself to architecture after 1839.

The Huguenot Church in Charleston was built to White's design in 1844–45. The vaulted ceiling is made of lath and plaster, and the buttress-crestings, gable ends and tracery of the principal window are all made of cast iron. The main part of the church is separated from the entry by a pierced wood screen of sliding panels within a framework of pointed arches, a clever but completely un-medieval device.

Huguenot Church, interior.

In 1845, White designed the German Artillery Hall on the south side of Wentworth Street between King and Meeting streets, Charleston. It was to be a meeting place for a part of the South Carolina militia. The cornerstone was laid in September, 1845, and the building was completed in 1847. The hall had a T-shaped plan, drip mouldings, pointed and Tudor arches, octagonal towers and crenellated parapets with bartizans. The Hall was demolished in 1930.

Above: German Artillery Hall, Wentworth Street, Charleston, 1845–47. *South Carolina Historical Society.* Below: Trinity Episcopal Church, 1100 Sumter Street, Columbia, 1845–57, transept and chancel added 1861–62. *South Caroliniana Library, University of South Carolina*

White designed Trinity Episcopal Church, Columbia, built between 1845 and 1847. It is a stuccoed brick structure with symmetrical western towers, shallow central entrance porch and large tracery window in the gable. Its interior has an arch-braced tie beam and king post ceiling with pendants at the crossing. The transepts and chancel were added in 1860–62 from White's original designs. Minor additions were made in 1893–98, and the chancel was remodeled in 1907. Other Gothic churches designed by White are Grace Church, 100 Wentworth Street, Charleston, 1847–48, the Episcopal Church, Walterboro, 1850, and the Chapel of the Cross, Bluffton, 1857.

In the late 1840's White participated in the design of the Graniteville Company, one of the most intriguing social, industrial and architectural experiments of the era. William Gregg was a Pennsylvania orphan who had learned the watchmaker's craft from his uncle and later became a prosperous South Carolina merchant. Gregg came to believe that the South was being ruined by its devotion to slaves and cotton and that cotton mills could help diversify the economy, employ landless whites, utilize the region's natural resources and end its dependence on slavery. So in 1846 Gregg organized, near the Charleston-Hamburg railroad outside Aiken, the Graniteville Company, which promised to employ several hundred workers producing 14,000 yards of cotton cloth a day.

Gregg wanted Graniteville to be a model community, where good architecture would be a force for moral improvement. In July, 1846, Gregg asked Richard Upjohn, English-born architect of New York's Trinity Church, for help: "I should like . . . to decide on some cheap stile of Architecture, that we may . . . build up a uniform Village conforming to some sort of order."[4] How could he build, Gregg asked, attractive but cheap workers' houses, each sixteen by thirty feet, with a single brick chimney and unfinished interior? By the spring of 1848, the mill village was ready—with factory, dams, waterways, landscaped malls, hotel, academy, churches and forty "cottages of the Gothic order of architecture . . . after handsome Architectural plans."[5] Upjohn designed the Baptist Church, E. B. White designed the Methodist Church, but the designer of the cottages is not known. All these buildings were board-and-batten frame buildings with tall gables and decorated bargeboards.

Academy and mill house at Graniteville Company, Graniteville, c. 1848.

In 1854, White made additions to the old Citadel in Charleston. In 1825, after a slave insurrection, alarmed authorities had begun construction of a state arsenal. Its design has been attributed to Frederick Wesner (1788–1848) but may have been the work of Robert Mills, who described the building in 1826: "An extensive citadel, or fortified arsenal and barracks, is now erecting at the upper end of the city . . .

where the principal stand of arms, &c. will be kept. The works will be guarded by bastions at the four angles, on which cannon will be mounted —the whole surrounded by a high wall."[6] The original two-story building, with its wooden crenellated parapet and high, small windows, was

Right: Citadel, Charleston, a building of 1825–29 enlarged 1849 and 1854. This early photograph shows the building before a fourth story was added in 1910. *South Caroliniana Library, University of South Carolina.* Below: Unitarian Church, Archdale Street, Charleston, remodeled in Gothic style between 1852 and 1854. *South Carolina Historical Society*

intended for actual defense against civil disorder. (After completing the Citadel, Wesner became captain of the Municipal Guard, a police force which patrolled the streets at night for slaves out after curfew, and later became master of the Work House, the Negro prison.) But after the building was converted into a military academy in 1842, its battlemented architecture became symbolic rather than practical. In 1849, White designed east and west wings and a third story for the main building, whose exterior was remodeled in more romantic medieval style, executed by 1854. A fourth story was added to the main building in 1910. White moved to New York in 1879 and died there in 1882.

Francis D. Lee was born in Charleston in 1826. He graduated from the College of Charleston in 1846 and began the study of architecture in the office of Edward C. Jones in 1849. Between 1852 and 1857, Jones and Lee worked in partnership. Lee, whose designs before and after the partnership were characteristically in the Gothic Revival, was probably responsible for the firm's essays in that style.

Between 1852 and 1854 Lee supervised the remodeling of the old Unitarian Church on Archdale Street, originally built between 1774 and 1787, installing a lath-and-plaster fan-vaulted ceiling and wooden Gothic window tracery. In May, 1859, the cornerstone was laid for St.

Unitarian Church, Archdale Street, Charleston, interior of 1852–54.

St. Luke's Episcopal Church, 22 Elizabeth Street, Charleston, 1859–62, interior view.

Above: Jail, Walterboro, 1855–56.
Below: Jail, Orangeburg, 1857–60.

Farmers' and Exchange Bank, 141 East Bay Street, Charleston, 1853. *Photograph by Frances Benjamin Johnston: Library of Congress*

Luke's Church, Charleston. Designed by Lee, its plan was a Greek cross with thirty-seven-foot-high windows at each of its four ends. A 210-foot-high tower was to have been built between the north and west arms of the cross, and the walls are still unfinished where it was intended. A fan-vaulted ceiling and balconies are supported by clustered columns. Though still incomplete, the church was consecrated in February, 1862.

The firm of Jones and Lee produced Gothic county jails at Walterboro, 1855–56, and Orangeburg, 1857–60, each with battlements and turrets. Louis J. Barbot, who had worked in Jones's office, and John H. Seyle, Barbot's partner between 1852 and 1856, remodeled the jail in Charleston in 1855. Several times enlarged since it was first built about 1802, Barbot and Seyle gave the old building its present Gothic appearance and added the octagonal wing, long attributed to Robert Mills.

In 1853, Lee designed the Farmers' and Exchange Bank at 141 East Bay Street, Charleston, in a fantastic mélange of styles which has been variously described as Gothic, Moorish, Persian and Hindu but was described at the time as "Saracen." Behind a brownstone façade, with horseshoe arches, a paved vestibule led into a two-story banking room lit by a skylight. The great room was twenty-one feet wide, forty-eight feet long and twenty-nine feet high and "finished in the most elaborate manner, Moorish arches, panels, brackets, arabesques . . . fresco painting . . . lighted by a glass paneled ceiling."[7] This dramatic room has, alas, been decapitated by the addition of a second floor. The Farmers' and Exchange Bank was completed in 1854.[8] Lee was also the probable designer of a fish market at the foot of Market Street, another Moorish design, completed in 1856. Granite steps led from a boat basin to a cast-iron structure, forty-five feet square.[9] Francis D. Lee moved to St. Louis in 1868 and died there in 1885.

Trinity Episcopal Church, Abbeville, was designed by George E. Walker in 1855. Walker (1826–1863) was a civil engineer and surveyor who had worked as assistant supervising architect at the Charleston Custom House in 1853 and as supervising architect of the State House in Columbia in 1854–55.[10] The cornerstone of Trinity Church was laid in 1859, and the building was consecrated in November, 1860. Stucco over brick, the building has a central entrance tower, pinnacled buttresses and battlements. The chancel window was made in England and delivered in 1863, despite the Civil War blockade of Charleston harbor.

Romantic, picturesque and exotic buildings were also designed in the Italian Villa style, inspired by the rural architecture of the north Italian countryside. It was first prominently used by John Nash in Regency England. Downing published Italian villas as well as Gothic cottages in

Farmers' and Exchange Bank,
141 East Bay Street, Charleston, 1853, two interior views.
Library of Congress

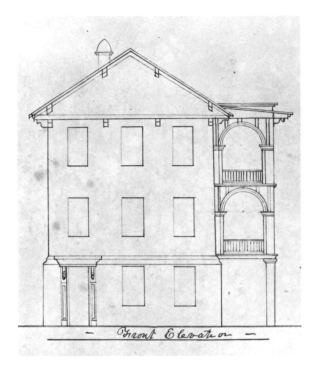

Drawing of house at 216 Ashley Avenue,
Charleston, c. 1850. *South Carolina
Historical Society*

his books of the late 1840's and early 1850's. Though he preferred the former to the latter, the Italian Villa style was easier to build than the Gothic and thus became the more popular style. Italian villas were asymmetrical, often with a tall tower and arcaded porches. Roofs were low, with wide overhanging eaves, supported by brackets, and a cupola or lantern. Round-headed windows were often grouped in twos or threes and embellished with heavy hood mouldings or pediments. Many of these same decorative elements, expressed with greater formalism, symmetry and grandeur, were used in the Renaissance Revival style of the same era.

In South Carolina, there are few true Italian Villa or Renaissance Revival buildings, but builders did adopt elements of those styles, especially wide, bracketed eaves and round-headed windows. An architect's drawing for a house, still standing at 216 Ashley Avenue in Charleston, was typical of that city, except its piazza, which had wide eaves, brackets and arches. Tidalholm, built for Edgar Fripp at Beaufort about 1856, was a real Italian villa, with an asymmetrical tower, before it was altered by a subsequent owner. The house of Colonel John Williams, at 544 Ball Drive in Laurens, is another Italian villa but with Greek Revival elements as well.

Tidalholm, 1 Laurens Street, Beaufort,
c. 1856, showing its original Italianate
exterior. *South Carolina Historical Society*

Edward C. Jones of Charleston was born in 1822, the son of a Charleston Custom House employee. In 1838, at the age of sixteen, he determined to become an architect. Apprenticed to builder James Curtis, he studied drawing for "a month or two" with a Professor Guthrie, his only formal architectural training.[11] During a partnership with his former pupil Francis D. Lee, Jones seems to have been responsible for the Italianate designs of the firm. Jones was probably the designer of the Colonel A. S. Ashe House, 1853, with its two-tiered arcaded porches, and the State Bank, at 1 Broad Street, a brownstone palazzo, both in Charleston.

In July, 1852, Jones wrote to Matthew Richard Singleton of Richland County: "I have connected myself in business with Mr. F. D. Lee of this city, and, as it is likely that I will be absent from the city most of the summer, I thought it best for him to take charge of your work."[12] Since May, 1852, Jones had been at work on plans for Kensington, a Renaissance Revival villa in lower Richland County, about twenty-five miles east of Columbia, for Matthew Richard Singleton, a planter who raised imported cattle, African brown-tailed sheep and race horses. In July, Lee visited the site and laid out the foundations. In August, Jones reported from Charleston that he had "ransacked the city" to locate a builder to supervise the work and found a Mr. Spears, who had been erecting a new store at the corner of Market and King streets, and a planing machine was purchased in New York so lumber could be dressed. In November, Jones reported, apologetically: "Our draughtsman brought in the plans to-day." By September, 1853, the building's framework was ready for a tin roof. In October, window sashes were ordered from New York. In January, 1854, painting began.[13]

Kensington is a two-story frame structure over an elevated brick basement, surrounded by arcaded porches and porte cochère with Corinthian pilasters. The visitor enters a two-and-one-half-story domed hall with skylight and second-story balcony enclosed by an iron rail cast in the form of giant acanthus leaves and anthemia. The hall leads through a passageway, with apsidal niches for statuary, to a long dining room with a coffered, barrel-vaulted ceiling. The brick-paved basement holds a cistern. The second-story rooms are awkwardly arranged under the low roof. Bedrooms had marble basins, supplied with hot water from a tank, and servants' bells or speaking tubes. The architect specified: "The exterior of the whole building will be painted of a warm drab stone Colour, weatherboarding, windows & door frames & Blinds. . . . Tin roof to be painted at present one coat of Spanish Brown paint."[14]

Colonel A. S. Ashe House, South Battery, Charleston, 1853.

Kensington, Richland County, 1851–53. Exterior view of 1983 exterior appearance.
Photograph by Russell Maxey. Opposite: Plan of Kensington.

ORPHAN HOUSE

Charleston Orphan House, E. C. Jones's drawing of proposed enlargements, c. 1853. *City of Charleston*

Wofford College, 509 North Church Street, Spartanburg, 1851, 19th century photograph. *Wofford College*

Between 1853 and 1855, Jones supervised the enlargement of the Charleston Orphan House, originally built between 1792 and 1794. Jones presented "Plans and Diagrams" for his proposed enlargements and improvements to the commissioners in January, 1853.[15] Wings and new central rooms were to be added, with a new entrance with arcaded Corinthian columns, similar to motifs used at Kensington. Work began in June, 1853, and was completed in October, 1855.

Jones designed the main building at Wofford College, at 509 North Church Street in Spartanburg, in 1851. It was to be a three-story stuccoed brick structure, with Corinthian portico and twin flanking towers, containing a chapel, museum, library, chemistry laboratory, recitation halls and professors' rooms. But the building contract, dated July, 1852, imposed some economies on the architect's original specifications: now the foundations were to be one foot shallower, the portico's steps and floor to be of wood instead of stone, the exterior walls were to be left plain instead of stuccoed, the handrails were to be made of walnut instead of mahogany, the nails were to be smaller and cheaper, and the columns of the portico were to have "Dorrick" instead of Corinthian capitals. The building was completed in August, 1854. Jones also designed the South Carolina Institution for the Deaf and Blind at nearby Glenn Springs for a school established by a young Baptist minister in 1849. The main block, with its Corinthian portico, is connected to wings by arcaded hyphens. The central building and east wing were built between 1857 and 1859, and the west wing was added by Samuel Sloan (who also added wings to Robert Mills's Insane Asylum) in 1884. Edward C. Jones moved to Memphis in 1866 and died there in 1902.

Orson Squire Fowler (1809–1887) was a phrenologist, vegetarian, teetotaler, sex educator and publisher whose exotic, quixotic architectural ideas appealed to the emotional age in which he lived. In his treatise, *A Home for All, or the Gravel Wall and Octagon Mode of Building*, 1853, Fowler looked to the natural world for his building ideas. Like nature's own favorite shapes—fruits, eggs, nuts, seeds and tree trunks—Fowler believed that houses should be spherical—or, next best, octagonal—in plan. He promised that octagonal buildings would be "several hundred percent. cheaper than any other." Similarly, walls should be erected with nature's own building materials—lime, stones and sand—which would be "simple, durable, easily applied, everywhere abundant, easily rendered beautiful, comfortable and every way complete." Singlehandedly, Fowler popularized a completely new style of domestic building in America.[16] But these octagonal buildings were architectural mules, without legitimate ancestry or hope of offspring.

South Carolina Institution for the Deaf and the Blind, Glenn Springs, 1857–59.

One of South Carolina's most extraordinary houses is Captain James Frazier's octagonal house at Cedar Springs, built between 1852 and 1856. A visitor described it in July, 1857: "A massive brick structure of octagon form, it rises like some castellated tower of the Middle Ages to the height of three stories. . . . It has been four years in the process of erection, and now that it is complete, is an ornament to the surrounding country."[17] The house is planned around three octagonal, stuccoed brick towers, connected by porches and hallways which surround the central tower, with a rectangular two-story projection at the rear. The principal room of the first story is ornamented with Gothic mantel and cupboards, the exterior with drip mouldings over windows, the porches with sawwork balusters. The structure appears to have been modified during construction or shortly after its completion, for the third story of the central octagonal tower has windows facing into the inside hall and its walls are finished with drip mouldings and cornice, as if intended to be open to the weather, and there is no entrance into the top story chamber except from an outside porch. Perhaps the top story, now mostly enclosed with hallways, was originally intended to be a wide open-air promenade, overlooking the neighborhood, with the tower chamber a kind of teahouse for this roof garden?

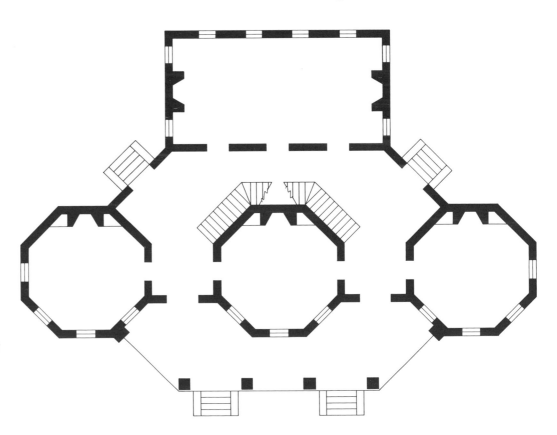

James Frazier House, Cedar Springs, 1852–56.

James Frazier House, exterior view.

James Frazier House, interior view.

Zelotes Lee Holmes, a Presbyterian clergyman, came to South Carolina from Sheridan, New York, in the 1840's and became professor of mathematics and natural philosophy at the Laurens Female College. His land in Laurens was surveyed in early November, 1857, and construction of an octagonal house begun late in 1858.[18] Walls, eighteen to twelve inches thick, rest on five-foot granite slabs and are made with large rocks and concrete-like mortar. By January, 1859, the basement and half of the structure was up, and the Holmes family was living in four completed rooms. The dwelling was essentially finished by the end of the year. The exterior was stuccoed, scored and painted to imitate stone. Its method of construction and octagonal shape seem to have been inspired by Orson Fowler, but the specific plan, with its projecting corner rooms, four porches and central hall, seems to have been copied from Samuel Sloan's *The Model Architect*, 1852. Sixteen chimneys, their shafts and tops arranged eccentrically, enliven the roof. A two-story hall at the center of the house rises some thirty-five feet to a skylight, with two balconies serving as passages between the rooms of the second story. Jib windows lead to the porches from the two principal rooms of the first story.

Zelotes Lee Holmes House, Laurens, 1858–59.

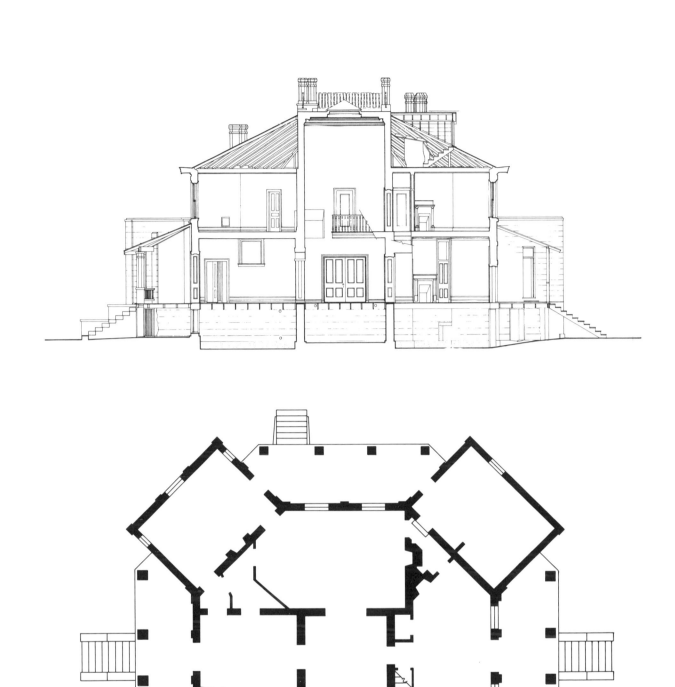

Zelotes Lee Holmes House.
Section from Library of Congress

In December, 1851, the building of a new fireproof building for state records was commenced at Columbia. In December, 1853, these plans were enlarged by P. H. Hammerskold, a Charleston architect of Swedish parentage, to encompass a new state capitol. In May, 1854, when cracks were discovered in the partially completed walls, Hammerskold was discharged. In late 1855 construction was resumed with a new architect, John Rudolph Niernsee (1831–1885), who came from Austria by way of Baltimore, and a new design, a massive granite building in Renaissance Revival style. Micajah Adolphus Clark wrote in 1857: "I . . . went to see the Capitol, the State House, now being erected. It is a very costly and magnificent building—about 300 feet long, building out of Granite Rock, which they procure some three miles from the State House. There was a Rail Road built out to the Rock quarry, to bring in the Rock."[19] Construction proceeded with agonizing slowness. By October, 1857, the walls reached the top of the basement windows. A year later the walls reached the sills of the main floor windows, thirty-seven feet above ground. By October, 1859, the walls were sixty-five feet high. Construction continued fitfully during the Civil War, and the partially completed building was damaged by fire and artillery shells in the winter of 1865. The legislature met in the University of South Carolina's buildings until a temporary wood roof was put on the walls of the capitol in 1869. Construction was resumed in 1885, supervised by various architects, including Niernsee, his former partner and son. Frank Milburn of Charlotte designed the portico and incongruously slender dome in 1900. The State House was finally declared complete in 1907.

State House, Columbia, begun 1855. Left: Design of John Rudolph Niernsee, as published in *Harper's Weekly* in 1860. Right: Incomplete building with temporary wooden roof and without porticoes, c. 1870. *Both illustrations: South Caroliniana Library, University of South Carolina*

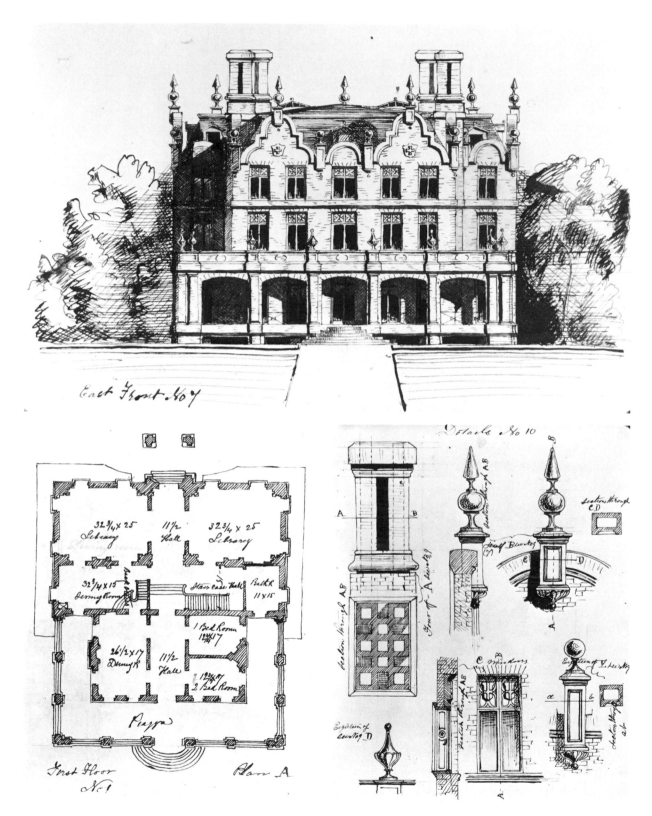

East Front No 7

Détails No 10

First Floor No 1   Plan A

Middleton Place, Ashley River, designs for improvements drawn by Fred J. Smith, 1863. *Middleton Place*

State House, completed 1907.

At the end of 1863, as the Civil War began to turn against the South, Williams Middleton, who had inherited Middleton Place in 1846, began to dream of improvements to his family's plantation on the Ashley River. It was a profound gesture of escape from the disastrous realities of a war which was destroying his way of life. Builder Fred J. Smith prepared drawings, dated December 29, 1863, for additions to the main house and alterations to the flankers. The house was to be more than doubled in size with additional rooms joined to the old structure and a new mansard roof. A new exterior was to be created in Jacobean Revival style, with clustered chimney stacks, curvilinear gables and casement windows. This style was used by Anthony Salvin, a pupil of John Nash and the recognized authority in mid-19th century England on medieval fortresses and castles. Middleton may have seen an example of the Jacobean Revival style, Spites Hall, published in the May 5, 1860, issue of the *Illustrated London News*. No improvements were made before Federal troops burned the main house and dependencies at Middleton Place in 1865. The property was rented to a "Yankee Captain" in 1866. Williams Middleton began repairs and returned to live in the rehabilitated southern flanker in 1871. With his intended romantic additions inspired by early English architecture, Middleton probably had sought to recreate a mood of permanence and stability which were destroyed by the war.

Middleton Place, the ruins after the Civil War. *Middleton Place*

Notes

Every student of South Carolina architecture should consult the following general works, to which this author is much indebted: "The Historic American Buildings Survey Catalogue, South Carolina," typescript, Washington, 1972; Harriette Kershaw Leiding, *Historic Houses of South Carolina* (Philadelphia, 1921); Samuel Gaillard Stoney, *Plantations of the Carolina Low Country* (Charleston, 1938); Beatrice St. Julien Ravenel, *Architects of Charleston* (Charleston, 1945); Alice R. and D. E. Huger Smith, *The Dwelling Houses of Charleston* (Philadelphia, 1917).

I. IN THE EARLY COLONY

1. South Carolina Historical Society, *Collections*, V (Charleston, 1897), pp. 147–149.
2. *South Carolina Historical and Genealogical Magazine (SCHM)*, XXXVII (1936), p. 55. After 1952, *SCHM* is titled *South Carolina Historical Magazine*.
3. *Ibid.*, p. 371.
4. A. S. Salley, Jr., *Records in the British Public Record Office Relating to South Carolina, 1664–1684* (Atlanta, 1928), p. 119.
5. *Ibid.*, p. 118.
6. Maurice Mathews, "A Contemporary View of Carolina in 1680" in *South Carolina Historical Magazine (SCHM)*, LV (1954), pp. 153–159.
7. Alexander Samuel Salley, *Narratives of Early Carolina* (New York, 1911), p. 181.
8. *Carolina Described More Fully than Heretofore* (Dublin, 1684), p. 27.
9. Agnes Leland Baldwin, *The First Settlers of South Carolina, 1670–1680* (Columbia, 1969).
10. [Thomas Nairne], *A Letter from South Carolina* (London, 1718), p. 45.
11. Ltr. of Margaret Kennett, January 20, 1725, in *SCHM*, LXI (1960), p. 15.
12. Nicholas Trott, *The Laws of the Province of South-Carolina* (Charles Town, 1736), p. 300.
13. Ltr. of Margaret Kennett, *op. cit.*, p. 15.
14. *South Carolina Gazette*, Charleston, September 4, 1736.
15. Thomas Nairne, *op. cit.*, p. 14.
16. John Lawson, *A New Voyage to Carolina* (London, 1709), p. 20.
17. *South Carolina Gazette*, Charleston, December 14, 1747.
18. *News and Courier*, Charleston, November 23, 1981.
19. Albert J. Schmidt, "Hyrne Family Letters" in *SCHM*, LXIII (1962), pp. 151, 153.
20. Quoted in *News and Courier*, Charleston, November 23, 1981.
21. Henry DeSaussure Bull, "Ashley Hall Plantation" in *SCHM*, LIII (1952), pp. 61–66.
22. Frank J. Klingberg, *The Carolina Chronicle of Dr. Francis LeJau, 1706–1717* (Berkeley, 1956), pp. 31, 65, 86, 98, 139–140, 192.
23. *Ibid.*, p. 98.
24. Anna Wells Rutledge, "The Second St. Philip's Church, Charleston, 1710–1835" in *Journal of the Society of Architectural Historians (JSAH)*, XVIII (1959), pp. 112–113.
25. George W. Williams, "Letters to the Bishops of London from the Commissaries" in *SCHM*, LXXVIII (1977), p. 25.
26. [George Milligen-Johnston], *A Short Description of the Province of South-Carolina* (London, 1770), pp. 32–33.
27. Little is known of the architect of the new church, Joseph B. Hyde, except that he offered classes in "Architectural Drawing and Mechanics." *Courier*, Charleston, October 24, 1836.
28. William B. Lees, "The Historical Development of Limerick Plantation" in *SCHM*, LXXXII (1981), pp. 44–62.
29. Elise Pinckney, *The Letterbook of Eliza Lucas Pinckney* (Chapel Hill, 1972), p. 61.
30. Duke de la Rochefoucauld-Liancourt, *Travels through the United States of North America* (London, 1799), I, p. 591.
31. *Ibid.*, p. 591.
32. "Middleton Place—From D. E. Huger Smith's Recollection," drawing by Langdon Cheves III, and "Measurements of Ruins, Middleton Place" by Samuel G. Stoney, in South Carolina Historical Society, Charleston.
33. *South Carolina Gazette*, Charleston, June 24, 1732.
34. *Ibid.*, February 17, 1733.
35. *Ibid.*, February 9, 1734.
36. *Ibid.*, January 11, 1735.
37. *Ibid.*, March 6, 1736.
38. *Ibid.*, July 17, 1736.
39. *Ibid.*, June 2, 1739.

II. GEORGIAN GRANDEUR

1. Charles Mackay, *Life and Liberty in America* (London, 1859), p. 204.
2. J. H. Easterby, *The South Carolina Rice Plantation as Revealed in the Papers of Robert F. W. Alston* (Chicago, 1945) and James M. Clifton, *Life and Labor on Argyle Island: Letters and Documents of a Savannah River Rice Plantation* (Savannah, Georgia, 1978) contain interesting documents of rice planting, useful introductions and extensive bibliographies.
3. Robert Mills to Eliza Mills, March 6, 1821 in *SCHM*, XXXIX (1938), p. 120.
4. Division of State Parks, South Carolina Department of Parks, Recreation and Tourism, "A Master Plan for Hampton Plantation State Park," typescript, Columbia, 1979.

5. James Glen, *A Description of South Carolina* (London, 1761), p. 5.

6. T. P. Harrison, *Journal of a Voyage to Charleston in South Carolina by Pelatiah Webster in 1765* (Charleston, 1898), p. 5.

7. *A Catalogue of Books belonging to the Incorporated Charleston Library Society* (Charleston, 1770).

8. See George C. Rogers, *Charleston in the Age of the Pinckneys* (Norman, 1969).

9. Josiah Quincy, *Memoir of the Life of Josiah Quincy Jun. of Massachusetts* (Boston, 1825), p. 73.

10. Frank Winkler Ryan, Jr., "Travellers in South Carolina in the Eighteenth Century" in *Yearbook of the City of Charleston* (Charleston, 1948), p. 219.

11. Bernhard Alexander Uhlendorf, *The Siege of Charleston . . . Diaries and Letters of Hessian Soldiers* (Ann Arbor, 1938), p. 327.

12. Joseph W. Barnwell, "The Diary of Timothy Ford, 1785–1786" in *SCHM*, XIII (1912), p. 142–143.

13. Elise Pinckney, *Letterbook of Eliza Lucas Pinckney* (Chapel Hill, 1972), p. 7.

14. James Glen, *op. cit.*, p. 180.

15. Journal of Josiah Quincy in Massachusetts Historical Society, *Proceedings*, XLIX (1916), p. 442.

16. *South Carolina Gazette*, Charleston, August 9, 1774.

17. John Bennett, "Charleston in 1774 as Described by an English Traveller" in *SCHM*, XLVII (1946), pp. 179–180.

18. Thomas J. Tobias, "Charles Town in 1764" in *SCHM* (1966), pp. 67–68.

19. Henning Cohen, "Four Letters from Peter Timothy" in *SCHM*, LV (1954), pp. 160–165.

20. Joseph W. Barnwell, *op. cit.*, p. 141.

21. *South Carolina Gazette*, Charleston, May 24, 1770.

22. [George Milligen-Johnston], *A Short Description of the Province of South-Carolina* (London, 1770), p. 35.

23. *South Carolina Gazette*, Charleston, January 19, 1765.

24. *Ibid.*, May 28, 1744.

25. *Ibid.*, May 16, 1748.

26. *Ibid.*, April 30, 1750.

27. *Ibid.*, May 20, 1751.

28. *Ibid.*, August 11, 1759.

29. *Ibid.*, March 14, 1768.

30. *Ibid.*, May 29, 1742.

31. *Ibid.*, July 14, 1767.

32. *Ibid.*, January 21, 1772.

33. George Rogers, *The Papers of Henry Laurens*, IV (Columbia, 1968), pp. 379, 395, 447, 555.

34. *South Carolina Gazette*, Charleston, November 1, 1773.

35. *Ibid.*, June 23, 1767, October 8, 1768, March 6, 1767, July 24, 1769, March 30, 1772.

36. William Bynum, *Drayton Hall, An Annotated Bibliography* (Washington, 1978).

37. John Davis, *Travels of Four Years and a Half in the United States of America* (New York, 1803), p. 116.

38. Alice R. and D. E. Huger Smith, *The Dwelling Houses of Charleston* (Philadelphia, 1917), pp. 361–373.

39. *South Carolina Gazette*, Charleston, February 17, 1752.

40. George W. Williams, *St. Michael's, Charleston, 1751–1951* (Columbia, 1951).

41. James Silk Buckingham, *The Slave States of America* (London, 1842), I, p. 560.

42. [George Milligen-Johnston], *op. cit.*, pp. 33–34.

43. Anne Alston Porcher, "Minutes of the Vestry of St. Stephen's Parish, South Carolina, 1754–1873" in *SCHM*, XLV (1944), pp. 164–165, 170.

44. Massachusetts Historical Society, *Proceedings*, XLIX (Boston, 1916), pp. 444–445.

45. Quoted in *Winterthur Portfolio III* (Winterthur, Delaware, 1967), p. 191.

46. *South Carolina Gazette*, Charleston, November 30, 1769.

47. Caroline Wyche Dixon, "The Miles Brewton House: Ezra Waite's Architectural Books and Other Possible Design Sources" in *SCHM*, LXXXII (1981), pp. 118–142.

48. *South Carolina Gazette*, Charleston, January 26, 1769.

49. *Ibid.*, November 23, 1769.

50. *Ibid.*, October 15, 1772.

51. *Ibid.*, November 1, 1773.

52. *Ibid.*, April 27, 1767.

53. Gene Waddell, "The Charleston Single House" in *Preservation Progress*, newsletter of the Preservation Society of Charleston, XXII, No. 2 (March, 1977), pp. 4–8.

54. Book R, pp. 246–251, August 13, 1789, in Land Records Miscellaneous, Part 87, Charleston County Courthouse. This reference comes, with others, from the research files of the Museum of Early Southern Decorative Arts, Winston-Salem, North Carolina.

55. Harriet P. and Albert Simons, "The William Burroughs House of Charleston" in *Winterthur Portfolio III* (Winterthur, Delaware, 1967), pp. 172–203.

III. ACROSS THE FRONTIER

1. Julian J. Petty, *The Growth and Distribution of Population in South Carolina* (Columbia, 1943) and Robert L. Meriwether, *The Expansion of South Carolina, 1729–1765* (Kingsport, 1940).

2. Richard J. Hooker, *The Carolina Back Country on the Eve of the Revolution, The Journal and Other*

Writings of Charles Woodmason (Chapel Hill, 1953), pp. 6, 7, 31, 121.

3. Robert Mills, *Statistics of South Carolina* (Charleston, 1826), p. 652.

4. P. J. Standenraus, "Letters from South Carolina, 1821–1822" in *SCHM*, LVIII (1957), p. 212.

5. Duke de la Rochefoucauld-Liancourt, *Travels through the United States of North America* (London, 1799), I, p. 592.

6. Robert Mills, *op. cit.*, gives brief descriptions of these villages.

7. D. H. Bacot, "South Carolina Up-Country at the End of the Eighteenth Century" in *American Historical Review*, XXVIII (1923), p. 692.

8. John Drayton, *A View of South-Carolina as Respects Her Natural and Civil Concerns* (Charleston, 1802), p. 111.

9. Richard Xavier Evans, "Letters from Robert Mills" in *SCHM*, XXXIX (1938), p. 110.

10. Colin Brooker, "Guillebeau House, McCormick County, South Carolina, Architectural and Archaeological Investigations," Upper Savannah Council, Greenwood, South Carolina, typescript, 1980. Kenneth E. Lewis, "The Guillebeau House: An Eighteenth Century Huguenot Structure in McCormick County, South Carolina," Institute of Archaeology and Anthropology, University of South Carolina, typescript, 1979.

11. The author is indebted to Martin Meek of Enoree, South Carolina, for this information.

12. "Caldwell-Hutchinson Farm," data pages, Historic American Buildings Survey, typescript, Washington, 1981.

13. "Journal of a Tour in the Interior of South Carolina" in *United States Literary Gazette*, November 15, 1825, pp. 104–108.

14. Frederick Law Olmsted, *A Journey in the Seaboard Slave States* (New York, 1856), pp. 384–385.

15. Stanley Smith, "Exploratory Excavations at the Price House," Institute of Archaeology and Anthropology, University of South Carolina, typescript, 1970.

16. Thomas D. Clark, *South Carolina: The Grand Tour* (Columbia, 1973), p. 39.

17. *City Gazette and Daily Advertiser*, Charleston, May 4, 1790.

18. Joseph A. Hoskins, *President Washington's Diaries, 1791 to 1799* (Summerfield, North Carolina, 1921), p. 37.

19. J. Franklin Jameson, "Diary of Edward Hooker" in *Annual Report of the American Historical Association* (Washington, 1897(, I, p. 854.

IV. THE FEDERAL STYLE

1. Thomas D. Clark, *op. cit.*, p. 35.

2. Robert Mills, *Statistics of South Carolina* (Charleston, 1826), p. 427.

3. Estate Appraisal of Richard Bohum Baker, November 8, 1785, in Baker-Grimké Papers, South Carolina Historical Society, Charleston.

4. *Times*, Charleston, August 18, 1801.

5. *City Courier*, Charleston, December 1, 1803.

6. Solomon Breibert, "The Synagogues of Kahal Kadosh Beth Elohim" in *SCHM*, LXXX (1979), pp. 215–235.

7. *Carolina Gazette*, Charleston, November 13, 1800.

8. Margaretta P. Childs, "America's City Halls: Entry from Charleston, South Carolina," City of Charleston, typescript, 1981, in South Carolina Historical Society.

9. Henry A. M. Smith, "Goose Creek" in *SCHM*, XXIX (1928), pp. 167–174.

10. Julian Boyd, *The Papers of Thomas Jefferson*, XII (Princeton, 1955), pp. 338–339, and XIII (Princeton, 1956), pp. 372–374.

11. John Hammond Moore, "The Abiel Abbot Journals, 1818–1827" in *SCHM*, LXVIII (1967), pp. 135–137.

12. Margaret Izard Manigault to Alice Izard, March 16, 1812, Manigault Family Papers, South Caroliniana Library, University of South Carolina, Columbia.

13. Anne Izard Deas to Mrs. Manigault, June 13, 1813, in Manigault Papers, South Caroliniana Library, University of South Carolina, Columbia.

14. Samuel Lapham, Jr., "Vanderhorst Row, Charleston, South Carolina" in *Architectural Forum*, XXXIX (August, 1923), pp. 59–61.

15. Margaret Manigault to Alice Izard, February 19, 1809, in Izard Papers, Library of Congress. Quoted in George C. Rogers, *Evolution of a Federalist* (Columbia, 1962), p. 383.

16. William Faux, *Memorable Days in America* (London, 1823), p. 43.

17. John Drayton, *A View of South-Carolina as Respects Her Natural and Civic Concerns* (Charleston, 1802), p. 111.

18. Basil Hall, *Travels in North America* (Edinburgh, 1829), pp. 139–140.

19. Nicholas Trott, *The Laws of the Province of South-Carolina* (Charles Town, 1736), p. 82.

20. [George Milligen-Johnston], *A Short Description of the Province of South-Carolina* (London, 1770), p. 31.

21. Thomas D. Clark, *South Carolina: The Grand Tour* (Columbia, 1973), p. 35.

22. Thomas T. Waterman, "A Survey of the Early Buildings in the Region of the Proposed Santee and Pinopolis Reservoir in South Carolina," National Park Service, Washington, typescript, 1939, in South Carolina Historical Society and Library of Congress.

23. Samuel Gaillard Stoney, *Plantations of the Carolina Low Country* (Charleston, 1938), p. 75.

24. Samuel G. Stoney, "Memoirs of Frederick Augustus Porcher" in *SCHM*, XLV (1944), p. 39.

25. Samuel Gaillard Stoney, *Plantations of the Carolina Low Country* (Charleston, 1938), p. 80.

26. Samuel G. Stoney, "Memoirs of Frederick Augustus Porcher" in *SCHM*, XLV (1944), pp. 35–36.

27. S. W. Johnson, *Rural Economy* (New Brunswick, 1806), p. 6.

V. ROBERT MILLS

1. M. Pierce Gallagher, *Robert Mills, Architect of the Washington Monument* (New York, 1935), p. 168.

2. John Morrill Bryan, *An Architectural History of the South Carolina College, 1801–1855* (Columbia, 1976).

3. *Ibid.*, pp. 42–43.

4. John Morrill Bryan, *Robert Mills, Architect, 1781–1855: An Unpublished Diary and Early Drawings* (Columbia, 1976), p. 11.

5. Benjamin H. Latrobe to Maximilian Godefroy, October 10, 1814, Latrobe Papers, Maryland Historical Society.

6. Robert Mills, *Statistics of South Carolina* (Charleston, 1826), p. 414.

7. John Hammond Moore, "The Abiel Abbot Journals, 1818–1827" in *SCHM*, LXVIII (1967), p. 70.

8. Robert Mills, *op. cit.*, p. 414.

9. Richard Yeadon, *History of the Circular Church* (Charleston, 1853), p. 13.

10. *Ibid.*, p. 12.

11. Emma Holmes Diary, December 16 and 17, 1861, Duke University Library.

12. George W. Williams, "Robert Mills's Contemplated Additions to St. Michael's Church, Charleston, and Doctrine of Sounds" in *JSAH*, XII (1953), pp. 23–32.

13. Samuel Lapham, Jr., "Architectural Specifications of a Century Ago" in *The Architectural Record*, LV (1923), pp. 239–244. The drawings and specifications are at the Charleston Library Society.

14. Robert Mills, *op. cit.*, p. 411.

15. David Bartling to James Chestnut, March 20, 1820. This and other documents are in Chestnut Family Papers, State Historical Society of Wisconsin, Madison.

16. Gene Waddell and Rhodri Windsor Liscombe, *Robert Mills's Courthouses & Jails* (Easley, South Carolina, 1982).

17. Specifications dated March 7, 1825, in South Carolina Department of Archives and History. Quoted by Waddell and Liscombe, pp. 49–50.

18. Robert Mills, *op. cit.*, p. 591.

19. *Ibid.*, p. 772.

20. Gene Waddell, "Robert Mills's Fireproof Building" in *SCHM*, LXXX (1979), pp. 105–135.

21. Robert Mills, *op. cit.*, p. 410.

22. Agreement between Mr. Gregory and the Commissioners of the Lunatic Asylum, March 2, 1827. Records of the State Treasurer, Bonds for Public Buildings, 1801–1844. South Carolina State Department of Archives and History.

23. Robert Mills, *op. cit.*, pp. 704–705.

24. Harold Cooledge, "Samuel Sloan," Ph.D. Dissertation, University of Pennsylvania, 1963.

25. Rodger E. Stroup, "The Robert Mills Historic House, Columbia, South Carolina" in *Antiques*, CXX (1981), pp. 1432–1440.

26. James C. Massey, "Robert Mills Documents, 1823: A House for Ainsley Hall in Columbia, South Carolina" in *JSAH* (1963), pp. 228–232.

27. *Courier*, Charleston, September 22, 1824.

28. Bess Glenn and A. S. Salley, *Some Letters of Robert Mills* (Columbia, 1928), p. 9.

29. Robert Mills, *Inland Navigation, Plan for A Great Canal* (Columbia, 1821).

30. Robert Mills, *Internal Improvement of South-Carolina, Particularly Adapted to the Low Country* (Columbia, 1822).

31. Robert Mills, Diary, December 27, 1828 to May 4, 1830, Tulane University.

32. Joseph I. Waring, "The Marine Hospitals of Charleston" in *Yearbook of the City of Charleston* (Charleston, 1939), pp. 172–183.

33. Robert Mills Papers, Robert Mills Notebook, Box 2, Library of Congress, pp. 107–109. These are discussed in John Morrill Bryan, *Robert Mills, Architect, 1781–1855: An Unpublished Diary and Early Drawings* (Columbia, 1976).

34. Roger Hale Newton, "Bulfinch's Design for the Library of Congress" in *The Art Bulletin*, XXIII (1941), pp. 220–222.

VI. THE GREEK REVIVAL

1. Gene Waddell, "The Introduction of Greek Revival Architecture in Charleston" in David Moltke-Hansen, *Art in the Lives of South Carolinians* (Charleston, 1979).

2. James Fenimore Cooper, *Home as Found* (Philadelphia, 1838).

3. Minute Book, October 3, 1837, Hibernian Society, microfilm in South Carolina Historical Society.

4. *Ibid.*, January 5, 1840.

5. *Courier*, Charleston, May 8, 1840.

6. *Ibid.*, January 22, 1841.

7. *Mercury*, Charleston, January 12, 1837.

8. *Ibid.*, March 21, 1840.

9. *Ibid.*, March 31, 1849.

10. William Ferguson, *America by River and Rail* (London, 1856), p. 109.

11. Manning to Potter, September 22, 1839, Williams-Chesnut-Manning Papers, Caroliniana Library, University of South Carolina.

12. Account Book, November 3, 1839, and November 17, 1840, in Williams-Chesnut-Manning Papers, Caroliniana Library, University of South Carolina.

13. "The Milford Papers" in Victorian Society *Newsletter*, 1974, pp. 1–4.

14. *Ibid.*

15. Minute Book, November, 1838 and October, 1839, Congregation Beth Elohim, Charleston.

16. The original is at the Synagogue, a typescript is included in Historic American Buildings Survey data pages, SC–81.

17. *Courier*, Charleston, March 20, 1841.

18. *Ibid.*, February 3, 1842.

19. *Ibid.*, September 21, 1838.

20. *Ibid.*, March 1, 1850.

21. Lois Craig, *The Federal Presence* (Cambridge, 1978), p. 107.

22. The author is indebted to Mrs. Richard Jones of Nashville, Tennessee, for biographical information about E. C. Jones, deposited at the South Carolina Historical Society, Charleston.

VII. ROMANTIC STYLES

1. *South Carolina Gazette*, May 12, 1767.

2. John Drayton, *A View of South-Carolina* (Charleston, 1802) discusses the backward state of manufacturing, pp. 149–150.

3. Tommy W. Rogers, "The Great Population Exodus from South Carolina" in *SCHM*, LXVIII (1967), pp. 14–21.

4. William Gregg to Richard Upjohn, July 14, 1846, Upjohn Collection, New York Public Library. See also letters of July 26, 1847, October 30, 1847, and June 17, 1848.

5. *Courier*, Charleston, March 17, 1848.

6. Robert Mills, *Statistics of South Carolina* (Charleston, 1826), p. 421.

7. *Courier*, Charleston, August 27, 1853.

8. *Ibid.*, July 1, 1854.

9. *Ibid.*, August 27, 1853.

10. See George E. Walker, "Architect's Diary, New State Capitol, Columbia, South Carolina," photocopy at South Carolina Historical Society, Charleston.

11. Biographical information, typescript at the South Carolina Historical Society.

12. E. C. Jones to Col. R. M. Singleton, July [n.d.], 1852, Singleton Family Papers, Southern Historical Collection, University of North Carolina, Chapel Hill. Singleton is also addressed as "M. R." Singleton.

13. E. C. Jones to Col. R. M. Singleton, May 7, 1852, and August 20, 1852; receipt dated August 5, 1852; Jones to Singleton, August 20, 1852, and November 25, 1852; estimate dated September 10, 1853; all, Singleton Family Papers.

14. Jones and Lee to Singleton, January 17, 1854, Singleton Family Papers.

15. Commissioners' Minutes, Orphan House, January 27, 1853, microfilm in South Carolina Historical Society.

16. Orson S. Fowler, *A Home for All, or the Gravel Wall and Octagon Mode of Building* (New York, 1853), pp. 3, 18.

17. *Independent Press*, Abbeville, July 3, 1857.

18. Martin E. Meek, "Z. L. Holmes' Octagonal House, Laurens, South Carolina," typescript, 1980.

19. Anne King Gregory, "Micajah Adolphus Clark's Visit to South Carolina in 1857" in *SCHM*, LIII (1952), p. 17.

Index